SINGER

SEWING REFERENCE LIBRARY®

THE
QUILTING BIBLE

COWLES
Creative Publishing, Inc.

Minnetonka, Minnesota, USA

SINGER

SEWING REFERENCE LIBRARY®

THE
QUILTING
BIBLE

Contents

The Quilting Bible draws pages from the
individual titles of the Singer® Sewing
Reference Library®. Individual titles are
also available from the publisher and in
bookstores and fabric stores.

Library of Congress
Cataloging-in-Publication Data
The quilting bible.
    p.   cm.
    Includes index.
    ISBN 0-86573-199-3. --
    ISBN 0-86573-200-0 (pbk.)
    1. Quilting. 2. Patchwork. I. Cowles
    Creative Publishing.
TT835.Q542 1997
746.46--dc21   97-19466

President: Iain Macfarlane
Executive V.P.: William B. Jones
Group Director, Book Development:
Zoe Graul

Created by: The Editors of
Cowles Creative Publishing, Inc.
Printed on American paper by:
R. R. Donnelley & Sons Co.
00 99 98 97/5 4 3 2 1

Introduction

We often marvel at the detailed workmanship and painstakingly tiny stitches of vintage quilts, wondering how our foremothers ever found the time to piece and quilt an entire project by hand! After all, they didn't have our modern conveniences to shorten their cooking, cleaning, and child care tasks. Granted, far fewer of them worked outside the home, but with farming chores, gardening, canning food, sewing and mending clothes, and raising large families, it is hard to imagine a leisurely moment devoted to such self-indulgence as decorative needlework.

Though today's technology has replaced elbow grease on the home front, careers and family and community involvement still leave us with precious little free time. Car pools, volunteer work, and recreational activities gobble up evenings and weekends. Long-term needlework projects are rarely started because we live in a world of instant gratification. We love the stress-relieving, creatively satisfying feeling of making something beautiful with our hands, but we want the finished product right now.

No wonder quilting by machine is so tremendously popular. With rotary cutting and quick-piecing methods, an entire quilt top can be stitched together in an evening. Machine-quilting techniques mimic hand-stitched quilting in a fraction of the time, with amazingly effective results. Short-term small projects, like wall hangings, table runners and placemats, baby quilts and lap quilts, and even mini quilts, provide creative enjoyment with far less time commitment. With machine quilting, even a bed-size quilt is no longer a lofty goal.

The Quilting Bible is designed as a comprehensive guide for machine piecing and quilting. In the Quilt Basics section, you are introduced to all the tools, terms, and techniques necessary to plan and complete any machine-quilting project. Instructions are photographed step-by-step to give you a clear picture of the quilt-making process, from selecting the fabric to hanging the finished quilt.

The project sections incorporate a wide assortment of block-pieced designs, including many traditional favorites like Log Cabin, Bow Ties, Drunkard's Path, Ocean Waves, and Ohio Star. For added inspiration, we show you different ways of arranging the quilt blocks to achieve interesting variations. There are also many contemporary designs and alternate piecing methods to help you fashion your own original quilt designs. You will find quilts for home decorating, quilts for comfort, and even quilted clothing and accessories. With such concise information and so many inspiring ideas, you will never run out of machine-quilting projects to enhance your leisure hours.

Quilt Basics

A Quilter's Vocabulary

Acid-free materials. Paper products, including tissue paper, cardboard tubes, and boxes, made especially for the storage of textiles. They do not contain the chemicals, normally found in wood and paper products, that can weaken and destroy fabric over time.

Appliqué. A cut fabric shape stitched to another piece of fabric.

Backing. Fabric used for the bottom layer of a quilt.

Batting. The middle layer of a quilt, which provides loft and warmth.

Bias. The diagonal of a piece of fabric. A true bias is at a 45° angle to both the lengthwise and crosswise grainlines of the fabric. The greatest amount of stretch in a woven fabric is on the true bias.

Binding. The strip of fabric used to enclose the edges of the three layers of a quilt.

Block. A square unit, usually made up of pieces of fabric sewn together in a design. Blocks are combined to make a quilt top.

Borders. Strips of fabric forming a frame around the quilt top. Borders may be plain or pieced.

Chainstitching. Sewing seams of several fabric pieces without breaking the stitching between the pieces. Also called chaining.

Fat quarter. A half-yard (0.5 m) of fabric, cut down the middle to measure 18" × 22" (46 × 56 cm). This is the equivalent of a quarter-yard (0.25 m) of fabric.

Free Motion Quilting. See freehand quilting.

Freehand quilting. Guiding the quilt through the sewing machine by using your hands, rather than pressure from the feed dogs and presser foot. Also called free motion quilting.

Lattice. See sashing.

Loft. The thickness and springiness of the batting.

Machine-guided quilting. Guiding the quilt through the sewing machine using pressure from the feed dogs and presser foot.

Medallion quilt. Quilt top with a central motif, usually framed by multiple borders.

Miter. To join corners at a 45° angle.

Piecing. Stitching together pieces of fabric to create a larger unit.

Quilt. A bedcover or wall hanging made by stitching together a top fabric, batting, and a backing fabric.

Quilting. Stitching through a top fabric, a batting layer, and a backing fabric in a design to add texture and to hold layers together.

Sampler quilt. A pieced quilt made up of many different block designs, rather than a single, repeated block design.

Sashing. Strips of fabric, plain or pieced, that divide the blocks in a quilt. Also called lattice.

Set. The way blocks are positioned in a quilt. They may be arranged in straight or diagonal rows.

Strip-piecing. Creating pieced designs from long strips of fabric by stitching the strips together, cutting them crosswise, and then stitching the pieces together to form the design.

Template. A pattern made of plastic or cardboard, used to trace cutting or stitching lines onto fabric.

Template-free. A method for cutting pieces using a ruler, instead of a template, as a guide.

Tied quilt. A quilt that is held together with ribbon or yarn, rather than with quilting stitches.

Anatomy of a Quilt

Freehand Quilting

Machine guided Quilting

Applique

Sashing

Border

Binding

Block

Batting

Backing

Selecting a Quilting Project

Start small and keep choices simple. Before making a full-size quilt, you may want to sew a smaller project that can be completed quickly, such as a pillow, table runner, or doll quilt. Before making a decision, it may be helpful to look through the entire book for more ideas.

You may want to experiment with several piecing techniques, using a different technique for each project. Or you can make a sampler quilt, using a different design for each block. You can also choose one block design for the entire quilt, varying the color and fabric.

Once you have decided on a project, you will need to make several other decisions, such as design, color,

Pillows

Doll quilt

Table runner

whether or not you want sashing or borders, and what type of binding you will use. It is not necessary to make all these decisions before you start your project, but it is helpful to have a basic plan in mind.

Choose template-free patterns. Template-free designs allow you to cut multiple pieces at one time and often allow you to use quick-piecing techniques. Designs that require templates must be traced individually onto fabric. They take more time to cut and are usually more difficult to assemble. Most of the patterns included in this book are template-free. Patterns are arranged in order, from designs that are easy to sew to those that are more difficult.

Crib quilt

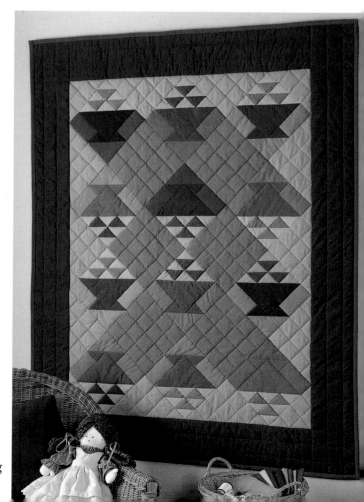

Wall hanging

Selecting a Design

Many quilters use a traditional quilt design rather than creating their own. This simplifies the design process. Study designs made by other quilters in order to see the effects of color, fabric, setting, and border variations.

Take your time selecting a design. Look at as many quilts, or photos of quilts, as possible. Quilt shops are a valuable source for design ideas. They generally carry an extensive selection of books and magazines and often have quilts on display.

Or, you may prefer to create your own design, rather than follow instructions from a book or magazine.

Shapes

Most piecing designs for quilt blocks are made up of one or more geometric shapes, such as squares, rectangles, triangles, and diamonds. Designs made up of curved shapes are less common, because they require more time and skill to construct. The more intricate curved shapes are usually appliquéd.

Block Designs

The most common type of quilt top is made up of blocks. A block is a pieced square of fabric. The number of squares that make a block can be four, nine, sixteen, twenty-five, or more. The pieces in the block may be identical, as in Patience Corner (opposite), which is made up of nine square pieces of fabric. Or they may be varied, as in Ohio Star (page 17), with triangles and squares creating the block, or Churn Dash (page 17), which is made up of squares, rectangles, and triangles. Some block designs, such as Log Cabin (opposite), do not divide into smaller squares.

The possible combinations for making blocks are infinite. Several different block designs can be stitched together to create a sampler quilt. But most quilt tops use a pattern of repeating blocks. The blocks may be arranged in many ways, called *settings* (pages 20 and 21), which can vary the overall quilt design.

Block Designs with Squares

Autumn Tints: 4-patch

Double Nine-patch: 9-patch

Patience Corner: 9-patch

Nine-patch: 9-patch

Puss in the Corner: 16-patch

Checkerboard: 16-patch

Block Designs with Rectangles

Roman Square: 4-patch

Chinese Coins

Streak O' Lightning: 9-patch

Courthouse Steps

Rail Fence: 4-patch

Log Cabin

Block Designs with Triangles

Yankee Puzzle: 4-patch

Card Trick: 9-patch

Birds in Air: 9-patch

Dutchman's Puzzle: 16-patch

Brown Goose: 16-patch

Lady of the Lake: 25-patch

Block Designs with Curves

Lafayette Orange Peel: 4-patch

Wheel of Fortune: 4-patch

Robbing Peter to Pay Paul: 16-patch

Queen's Crown: 16-patch

Wonder of the World: 16-patch

Vine of Friendship: 25-patch

Bright Hopes: 4-patch

Churn Dash: 9-patch

Rolling Stone: 9-patch

Ohio Star: 9-patch

Puzzle Boxes: 9-patch

Maple Leaf: 9-patch

Clay's Choice: 16-patch

Evening Star: 16-patch

Road to Oklahoma: 16-patch

Grandmother's Choice: 25-patch

Cake Stand: 25-patch

Crown of Thorns: 25-patch

Copying a Quilt Design

To copy a quilt design, isolate one block by finding where the design starts to repeat itself in each direction. Look at the entire quilt to see if all the blocks are the same; some quilts have two or more different block designs. When a quilt includes more than one design, it is necessary to draft each design separately. Quilts with blocks on a diagonal will also have half or quarter blocks to complete the quilt top.

Look at each quilt block to see how many squares it is divided into. Draw the block on a plain piece of paper or quilter's graph paper. Divide this block into squares, and then divide it again into smaller shapes. It is easier to copy blocks made up of squares, rectangles, or triangles; most diamonds and curved shapes require templates.

Identifying the Block Design

Examples of quilt designs include those made up of two or more block designs (left), one-block designs set on the diagonal with sashing (middle), or one-block designs set side by side (right). Each block breaks down into squares, rectangles, triangles, or a combination of shapes. Copy each different block design, opposite.

How to Draft a Quilt Block

1) Visualize a grid of equal squares on quilt block. The block may be divided into four, nine, sixteen, or more equal squares.

2) Determine desired finished size of the quilt block; choose a size that divides easily, such as 6", 9", or 12" (15, 23, or 30.5 cm) for a 9-patch block, or 8" or 12" (20.5 or 30.5 cm) for a 16-patch block. Draw a square on paper the size of finished block.

3) Divide each side of the square by the number of squares on each side of quilt block; mark grid.

4) Determine the smaller shapes that make up each square of the quilt block; draw corresponding horizontal, vertical, and diagonal lines.

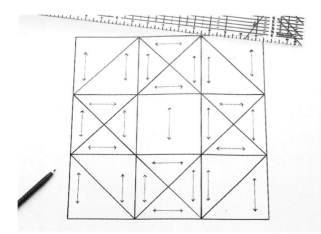

5) Mark grainline on each shape, parallel to outer edges, to use as a reference when cutting.

6) Measure finished size of each shape; cut pieces, adding seam allowances (pages 43 and 51).

Side-by-side settings are commonly used. Individual blocks are stitched together in rows. This makes the blocks blend together and may reveal an overall pattern.

Settings for Quilts

Blocks may be arranged in a number of ways, which are called settings, or sets. Changing the setting can make the same block design look different. When pieced blocks are placed side by side, design lines, such as squares or diagonals, may become evident. Placing sashing strips between blocks or alternating plain and pieced blocks can produce two entirely different looks. You can also place the blocks on their points, either with or without sashing. When designing a quilt, you may want to try a variety of settings, using many photocopies of the block design or the actual pieced blocks to determine the setting you like best.

Diagonal side-by-side settings are blocks stitched together in diagonal rows, so that blocks stand on their points. Often, a diagonal setting creates a sense of motion or appears to add curves to a pieced design.

Straight alternating block settings use pieced blocks alternating with plain blocks. The plain blocks reduce the amount of piecing required and provide space for freehand quilting stitches.

Diagonal alternating block settings are the same as straight alternating block settings, except the blocks are turned on their points.

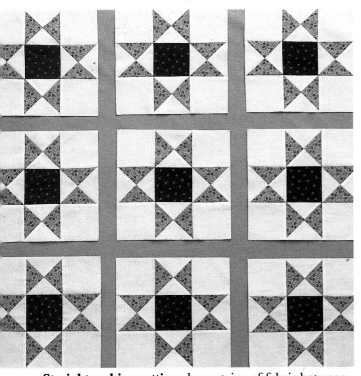

Straight sashing settings have strips of fabric between side-by-side blocks. This defines the individual blocks and provides a framework that unifies different block designs.

Diagonal sashing settings are the same as straight sashing settings, except the blocks are turned on their points.

Quilt Designs Without Blocks

Block designs are the most common designs, but there are many that cannot be broken down into blocks. One-patch quilts are made up of pieces that are all the same shape and size. Any shape can be used for a one-patch quilt. Medallion quilts have a central motif that can be pieced, appliquéd, or quilted. The motif is then surrounded by multiple borders. Many of these quilt designs require a template and specific piecing instructions.

Trip Around the World is a 1-patch quilt made up of squares.

Thousand Pyramids is a 1-patch quilt made up of triangles.

Carpenter's Wheel is a medallion quilt with a central motif surrounded by a larger motif.

Lone Star is a medallion quilt with a single central motif made up of small diamonds.

Borders for Quilts

A border is a fabric frame that surrounds a quilt. The color chosen for the border can highlight different designs and fabrics within the quilt. A quilt may have a single border or multiple borders of varied widths. Interrupted or pieced borders add interest and can repeat a design in the quilt or sashing.

Four Borders for Quilts

Single border is a fabric strip, of any width, stitched to the edges of the pieced design.

Multiple border is made of two or more borders of varied widths.

Interrupted border is broken by a small plain or pieced block, usually at the corners. A checkerboard unit (page 45) is frequently used.

Pieced border is made of randomly spaced pieces or of pieced strips, such as Flying Geese strips (pages 52 and 53).

Selecting Fabrics

Fabric is usually selected after a quilt design and color scheme have been chosen, although a special piece of fabric may help create a design idea or establish color for a quilt. Many kinds of fabric can be used for a quilt, but a primary consideration is fiber content.

Fabric of 100 percent cotton is the best choice for quilts. Cotton fabric is easy to cut, sew, and mark; it is also easy to press, holds a crease well, and is available in a wide range of colors and prints. The quality and weight of cotton fabric is determined by thread count. The thread count is the number of threads per inch (2.5 cm) of fabric. In high-quality cotton fabric, the thread count is equal lengthwise and crosswise; this is called an even weave. Most quilting cottons are either 78-square or 68-square. Fabrics with lower thread counts are too lightweight.

Cotton/polyester blends resist wrinkling and abrasion, making them a suitable choice for frequently washed quilts. The different lengthwise and crosswise thread counts in cotton/polyester blends cause a different amount of stretch along the lengthwise and crosswise grains, which can make it more difficult to piece fabrics accurately. Also, when stitched, cotton/polyester blends tend to pucker more than 100 percent cotton fabrics.

Choose good-quality fabrics that are compatible with the function of your quilt. If you are making a comforter for a child's bed, the quilt will be subject to hard and constant use; select fabrics that can withstand wear and frequent washing. If you are making a wall hanging, the durability of the fabric is less important.

Types of Quilting Fabrics

Quilting fabrics include calico, muslin, and other broadcloths. They are mediumweight, closely woven fabrics of 100 percent cotton or of a cotton/polyester blend. Calico (1) and other printed fabrics are available in a variety of patterns and colors. Muslin (2) is off-white or white, and is usually used for the background pieces in a pieced design, for the plain blocks, or for a quilt backing. Broadcloth (3) is a plain-weave fabric and is generally a solid color. Hand-dyed fabrics (4) are 100 percent cotton and are available in gradations of solid colors. These fabrics can be purchased from some quilting stores and from mail-order sources. Chintz (5) is a tightly woven fabric with a glazed finish and is usually 100 percent cotton. The shiny or glossy finish gives chintz its unique character, but it may wash out after a few launderings. The finish may cause the fabric to pucker when stitched. Pins and stitching may leave permanent holes, so care must be taken when piecing or basting quilts made from chintz fabrics.

Selecting Backing Fabrics

Select a backing fabric that has the same care requirements as the fabrics in the quilt top. Fabrics of 100 percent cotton are the best choice for machine quilting, because they do not pucker as much as cotton/polyester blends.

Some fabrics are manufactured specifically for quilt backing. They are 100 percent cotton and are available in 90" and 108" (229 and 274.5 cm) widths, so they

usually do not require piecing. These fabrics are available in light-colored prints on white backgrounds and a few solid colors. If the quilt will be finished with a mock binding (pages 110 and 111), choose a backing fabric that will coordinate with the quilt top.

Sheets are not a good choice for the backing fabric, because the permanent-press finish may cause skipped stitches and pucker the fabric.

Tips for Selecting Backing Fabrics

Solid-colored fabric accentuates the quilting stitches; printed fabric tends to hide the stitches.

Backing fabric should not show through to the quilt top when the batting has been sandwiched between the layers. If it does show through, change to a lighter-colored backing fabric.

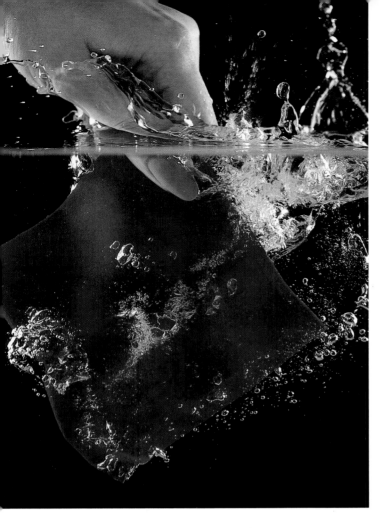

Preparing the Fabric

If you plan to wash the quilt, test dark or vivid-colored fabrics for colorfastness to determine whether the dye bleeds to light-colored fabrics or colors the water. If colors do bleed, repeat the test; if a fabric still bleeds, it is probably not colorfast.

Fabrics can be preshrunk by machine-washing them using a mild soap, such as dishwashing soap. Do not use soap intended for fine woolens; it may yellow cotton fabrics. Machine-dry the fabric, using a warm setting.

Preshrinking fabrics removes excess dyes and chemical finishes used in the manufacturing process. Most cotton fabrics shrink 2 to 3 percent when washed and dried, so if they are not preshrunk, the fabrics may pucker at the stitching lines and the finished size of the quilt may change the first time it is washed. After preshrinking, you may want to press the fabric, using spray starch, to make cutting and stitching easier.

Fabric is not always woven with the threads crossing at 90° angles; however, it is usually not necessary to straighten the grainline. Minor variations in the grainline do not change the overall look of a quilt block and straightening the grainline may waste as much as 4" (10 cm) of a piece of fabric.

How to Test Fabric for Colorfastness

1) Fill jar or glass with warm water and a few drops of mild soap, such as dishwashing soap.

2) Cut 2" to 6" (5 to 15 cm) square of fabric. Place in water. Allow to soak until the water has cooled slightly. Swish fabric.

3) Place wet fabric on sample of light-colored fabric for the quilt; blot dry. If dye transfers to light-colored fabric, repeat the test; if fabric still bleeds, it is probably not colorfast.

Selecting Batting

Batting is the middle layer of a quilt. The loft, or thickness, of the batting determines the warmth or springiness of the quilt. Batting is purchased according to the amount of loft desired (opposite).

The most widely used fibers for batting are cotton and polyester, or a blend of the two. Cotton batting gives a flat, traditional appearance when quilted. Polyester batting gives a puffy look and is more stable and easier to handle than cotton batting. Cotton/polyester batting combines the flat appearance of cotton with the stability and ease in handling of polyester.

Two types of batting are frequently used: bonded and needlepunch. Bonded batting is made by layering fibers and then adding a finish to hold the fibers together and make the batting easier to handle. Quilting stitches may be placed as far apart as 5" (12.5 cm). Needlepunch batting is made by layering the fibers and then passing them through a needling machine to give a dense, low-loft batting. It is firm, easy to handle, and warm. Most needlepunch batting is polyester.

The fibers in batting may migrate, or move, affecting the appearance of the quilt. Bonded batting is treated to help control fiber migration. There are two forms of fiber migration: bunching and bearding.

Bunching is the migration of fibers within a quilt, causing thick and thin areas. Bunching can be controlled by placing the quilting stitches ½" to 1" (1.3 to 2.5 cm) apart.

Bearding is the migration of fibers through the surface of the quilt. Polyester batting tends to beard, and these fibers may pill. Cotton batting may beard, but the fibers break off at the surface. To help prevent bearding, use a closely woven fabric for the quilt top and backing. If using a batting that may beard, avoid dark-colored fabrics, because the bearding is more noticeable on these fabrics. If bearding does occur, clip the fibers close to the surface of the quilt; do not pull the batting through the fabric. After clipping the fibers, pull the quilt top away from the batting so the fibers return to the inside of the quilt.

Batting is available in a wide range of sizes, although the selection in certain fibers and construction types may be limited. Polyester battings have the widest range of sizes and lofts. Batting should extend 2" to 4" (5 to 10 cm) beyond the edges of the quilt top on all sides, to allow for the shrinkage that occurs during quilting.

Batting is packaged for standard-size quilts. It is also available by the yard and in smaller packages for clothing and craft projects.

Guidelines for Selecting Batting

Fiber Content	Appearance of Finished Quilt	Characteristics	Spacing of Quilting Stitches
Cotton	Flat	Absorbs moisture, cool in summer and warm in winter	½" to 1" (1.3 to 2.5 cm)
Polyester	Puffy	Warmth and loft without weight, nonallergenic, moth and mildew-resistant	3" to 5" (7.5 to 12.5 cm)
Cotton/polyester Blend	Moderately flat	Combines characteristics of cotton and polyester	2" to 4" (5 cm to 10 cm)

Tips for Selecting Batting

Low-loft bonded cotton or cotton/polyester batting is easiest to handle.

Medium-loft adds texture to the finished quilt. The higher the loft, the more difficult to machine-quilt.

High-loft and extra-high-loft battings are best used for tied quilts, because they are difficult to machine-quilt.

Batting Thickness

Low-Loft	⅛" to ⅜" (3 mm to 1 cm)
Medium-loft	½" to ¾" (1.3 to 2 cm)
High-loft	1" to 2" (2.5 to 5 cm)
Extra-high-loft	2" to 3" (5 to 7.5 cm)

Packaged Batting Sizes

Crib	45" × 60" (115 × 152.5 cm)
Twin	72" × 90" (183 × 229 cm)
Full	81" × 96" (206 × 244 cm)
Queen	90" × 108" (229 × 274.5 cm)
King	120" × 120" (305 × 305 cm)

Determining the Finished Size

The first thing you must know in order to figure yardage requirements is the finished size of the quilt. If you are making the quilt for a bed, the finished size is determined either by the measurements of the bed or by the size of the packaged batting. If you are making the quilt to hang in a particular space, you can measure the space available.

To determine the finished size of a quilt by the bed measurements, measure the bed with the blankets, sheets, and pillows that will be used with the quilt. If you are using a thick batting, place the batting on the bed along with the bedding to ensure that the quilt will be large enough.

Measure the width of the bed from side to side across the top; do not include the pillows. Then measure the length of the bed from the head of the bed to the foot; if the quilt is to include a pillow tuck, include the pillow in the length measurement, tucking the tape around and under the pillow as you plan to tuck the finished quilt. A pillow tuck usually adds an additional 10" to 20" (25.5 to 51 cm) to the length, depending on the size and fullness of the pillows.

For the drop length, measure from the top of the bed to the desired length. For a comforter, measure to just below the mattress, about 9" to 12" (23 to 30.5 cm) down from the top of the bed. For a coverlet, measure to just below the box spring, about 18" (46 cm) down from the top of the bed. For a bedspread, measure to the floor, about 20½" (52.3 cm) down from the top of the bed. Add two times the drop length to the width of the bed for the two sides, and a single drop length to the length of the bed for the foot.

Determine the finished quilt size by the packaged batting sizes (page 29). Batting should be 2" to 4" (5 to 10 cm) larger on each side than the finished quilt. Packaged battings are usually sized for coverlets.

Adjust the finished measurements of the quilt according to the thickness of the batting and the amount of quilting you plan to do. For most average-size quilts with low or medium-loft batting, shrinkage due to quilting is about 2 to 3 percent. For high-loft batting, shrinkage may be 5 to 6 percent.

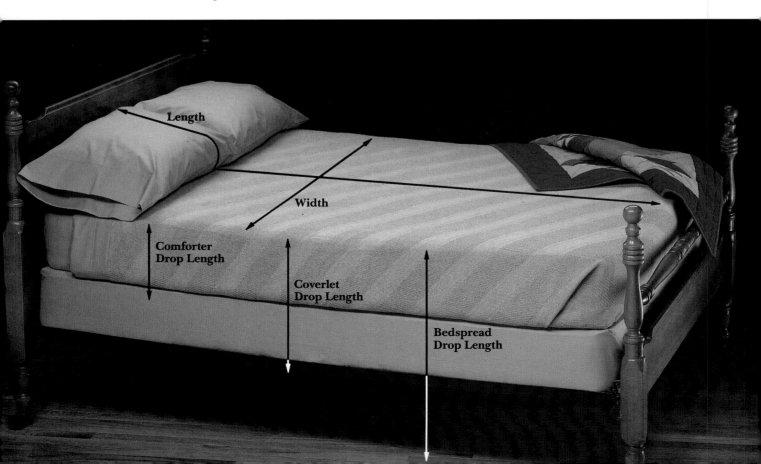

Backing Fabric

Yardage for backing fabric is based on the quilt top measurements and whether or not the backing will be seamed. Backing fabrics should extend 2" to 4" (5 to 10 cm) beyond the edges of the quilt top on all sides to allow for shrinkage during quilting.

Some fabrics are available in 90" and 108" (229 and 274.5 cm) widths, but most are 45" (115 cm) wide and will have to be seamed (page 95). It is helpful to make

a sketch of the quilt back, including seams, to calculate yardage. The information below is for 45" (115 cm) fabric with a usable width of about 40" (102 cm).

Crib quilts usually do not require seaming because they can be made from one width of backing fabric cut to the desired length. For crib quilts, allow only 1" to 2" (2.5 to 5 cm) on all sides for shrinkage during quilting.

How to Calculate Yardage for Backing Fabric

Quilt backings for twin-size quilts less than 80" (203.5 cm) long can be pieced horizontally for the best use of fabric.

Quilt backings 40" to 80" (102 to 203.5 cm) wide require seaming two widths of fabric together. The two widths can be seamed down the center of the quilt, or one of the widths can be cut and seamed to the sides.

Quilt backings wider than 80" (203.5 cm) usually require three widths of fabric seamed together. Or use two widths of fabric at the sides and piece a center panel from matching or contrasting fabrics.

Notions & Equipment

A few carefully selected notions can make quilting easier and help improve your accuracy in cutting, marking, and sewing.

Quilting can be done entirely on a straight-stitch conventional sewing machine. Choosing the correct type of sewing machine accessories, such as presser feet and needle plates, can help improve your results.

Measuring & Cutting Tools

See-through rulers **(1)** serve as both a measuring tool and a straightedge for cutting with a rotary cutter.

Measurements are visible through the ruler, so you can cut without marking. Many sizes and types of see-through rulers are available. A ruler 6" × 24" (15 × 61 cm) is recommended, because it is versatile.

Features of rulers vary widely. Some rulers are printed with measurements in two colors to show clearly on both light and dark fabrics. Some have a lip on one edge to hook onto the edge of the cutting mat for easier alignment. Some are printed on the underside to prevent distortion and increase accuracy; if the lines and numbers are molded on the underside, it will help prevent slippage. Square rulers, and rulers with 30°,

45°, and 60° angle lines, are available. Choose rulers that have the features most important for the type of quilting you are planning to do.

Suction rings **(2)** and suction handles **(3)** are available to help in positioning a ruler.

Rotary cutters **(4)** allow you to cut smooth edges on multiple layers of fabric quickly and easily. The cutters are available in various sizes: the smaller size works well for cutting curves or a few layers of fabric; the larger sizes work well for cutting long, straight edges or many layers of fabric.

Cutting mats **(5)**, made especially for use with rotary cutters, protect the blades and the table. They may be plain, or printed with a grid and diagonal lines. A mat printed with a grid is helpful for cutting right angles. Mats come in a variety of sizes. Choose a mat at least 22" (56 cm) wide to accommodate a width of fabric folded in half.

Sewing scissors **(6)** and shears **(7)** are used for cutting shapes and clipping threads. X-acto® knives **(8)** are used for cutting cardboard, paper, and plastic templates for pieced or appliquéd designs.

Marking Tools

The markings on a quilt should last only as long as you need them, and you should be able to remove them easily and thoroughly without damaging the quilt. Always test markers on fabrics to see how long the markings last and to be sure they can be removed. Mark lightly; it is more difficult to remove markings that are embedded in the fibers.

A special fabric eraser (1) can be used to remove light lead pencil (2) marks without abrading or leaving marks on the fabric. Oil-free and wax-free colored pencils (3) may also be used for marking. Choose a color close to the fabric color; or choose silver, because it shows on most fabrics. Remove marks before pressing the fabric or washing it in hot water; heat may set pencil marks. White water-soluble pencils (4) are available for marking dark fabrics; remove marks with a damp cloth. Soapstone pencils (5) are made of pressed talc and marks can be rubbed off or wiped off with water.

Chalk wheels (6) are available in a variety of shapes and colors; marking is fine and accurate. Chalk-wheel marks brush off easily, are washable, and will not stain.

A variety of plastic sheets (7) is available for making your own templates. Precut templates (8) are available for marking traditional quilting designs.

Sewing & Quilting Tools

For ease in stitching, thread should be of good quality. For piecing, use 100 percent cotton (1) or all-purpose sewing thread (2); match thread color to the darker fabric or use a neutral color, such as black, cream, or gray, to blend. For basting, use a fine, white cotton basting thread (3), or white all-purpose thread; the dye from dark thread could rub off on fabrics.

For quilting, 100 percent cotton thread is usually the best choice. Fine, .004 mm, or size 80 monofilament nylon thread (4), which comes in smoke or clear, is good for quilting and for invisibly stitching appliqués, because it blends with all colors. Cotton quilting thread (5) without a finish may be used for machine quilting; however, quilting thread with a special glacé finish should not be used for machine quilting. Quilting thread may either match or contrast with the fabric.

Insert a new sewing machine needle (6) before beginning a quilting project. For piecing and appliqué, use a size 9/70 or 11/80; for machine quilting, use a size 11/80 or 14/90 needle, depending on the thickness and fiber content of the batting.

Safety pins (7) are essential for pin-basting a quilt; 1" (2.5 cm) rustproof pins work well for most quilting projects. Use milliners needles (8) for thread-basting, because they are long and have small, round eyes. Use glass-head quilting pins (9), because they are long, 1¾" (4.5 cm), and strong.

Sewing Machine Equipment

A straight-stitch conventional sewing machine is used for quilting. The stitch length should be easy to adjust, because you start and end lines of stitches by gradually increasing or decreasing the stitch length.

An entire quilt can be made using only the straight stitch, but several additional features, common on most sewing machines, expand your quilting options. A blind-hem stitch can be used for attaching appliqués. Feed dogs that can be covered or dropped allow you to do freehand quilting.

Presser Feet

Special presser feet are not necessary for machine quilting, but they can improve your results. For machine-guided quilting, an Even Feed™ foot (1) is recommended for pucker-free stitching. The feed dogs on the Even Feed foot work with the feed dogs of the sewing machine to pull layers of fabric through at the same rate of speed. For freehand quilting, you can either use a darning foot (2) or stitch without a foot, depending on the sewing machine.

Use a general-purpose foot (3), or a special-purpose foot for zigzag and blindstitching. A straight-stitch foot (4) can improve the quality of stitches, particularly when piecing fabrics with the narrow seam allowances that are standard in quilting.

Needle Plates

Use a general-purpose needle plate (5) with the general-purpose or special-purpose foot for zigzag and blindstitching. Use a straight-stitch needle plate (6) with the straight-stitch foot for straight and uniform seams and quilting lines. The small hole in the needle plate keeps the fabric from being pushed down into the sewing machine as you stitch. Also use the straight-stitch needle plate with the Even Feed foot for machine-guided quilting and with the darning foot for freehand quilting.

The Work Area

The most important considerations in arranging a work area for machine quilting are comfort and convenience. Be sure the sewing machine is at a comfortable height, so that your shoulders are relaxed when you are quilting. If possible, choose a cutting surface approximately hip height. The cutting area should be able to accommodate about one yard (0.95 m) of fabric.

Position the sewing, pressing, and cutting areas so they are convenient to each other; be sure you have a good source of light over each area. Set up the iron and ironing board within easy reach, because seam allowances are pressed frequently during piecing.

A flannel board in a neutral color is valuable when you are designing a quilt. You may use felt or batting instead of flannel. When hanging the flannel board on a wall or door, make sure there is room to step back and view the total design. Use the board when determining how fabrics work together before stitching blocks, when judging the effect of different designs, or when evaluating various settings.

To make quilting easier, expand the sewing surface to support the fabric both to the left of and behind the sewing machine. The surface should be continuous and smooth, so the quilt will move freely, without catching. The surface should be at the same height as the bed of the machine, if possible. If you are using a free-arm sewing machine, convert it to a flatbed.

For a portable sewing machine, place the machine 5" or 6" (12.5 or 15 cm) in from the front edge, and allow enough room to the left of the machine to support the quilt.

Hang flannel, felt, or batting on a wall to serve as a flannel board when designing a quilt; fabric pieces will adhere without pins.

For a sewing machine in a cabinet, pull the cabinet away from the wall. Place one table behind it, and another under the leaf, to provide support for the quilt and to reduce strain on the hinges of the cabinet.

Basic Piecing Techniques

The designs in this section are for basic, traditional quilt patterns, and range from simple squares to more complex curves and appliqués. With the exception of curves and appliqués, the pieces are cut using template-free methods.

The techniques for setting up the sewing machine and for cutting, stitching, and pressing the fabrics are the same for most pieced designs.

Accuracy is critical to successful piecing. A small error can multiply itself many times, resulting in a block or a quilt that does not fit together properly. Check the accuracy of your cutting and stitching frequently. You may want to practice cutting and stitching techniques on a small project before using them on a large project.

Cutting Techniques

The quick-cutting techniques that follow are both timesaving and accurate. Instead of cutting each piece of the quilt individually, stack several layers of fabric and cut them into crosswise strips. The pieces are then cut from these strips, eliminating the need for templates.

Determine the grainline by folding the fabric in half and holding it by the selvages. Then shift one side until the fabric hangs straight. It is not necessary to straighten quilting fabrics that are off-grain or to pull threads or tear fabrics to find the grainline.

Good-quality cutting equipment helps ensure that every piece you cut is exactly the right size and that all the pieces fit together perfectly. Use a rotary cutter with a sharp blade and a cutting mat with a printed grid.

Tape three or four thin strips of fine sandpaper across the width of the bottom of a see-through ruler, using double-stick tape. This prevents the ruler from slipping when you are cutting fabric.

How to Cut Fabric Strips

1) Fold fabric in half, selvages together. Hold selvage edges, letting fold hang free. Shift one side of fabric until fold hangs straight. Fold line is straight of grain.

2) Lay fabric on cutting mat, with fold along a grid line. Place ruler on fabric close to raw edge at 90° angle to fold. Trim along edge of ruler, taking care not to move fabric. Hold ruler *firmly*; apply steady, firm pressure on blade. Stop when rotary cutter gets past hand.

3) Leave blade in position; reposition hand ahead of blade. Hold firmly and continue cutting. Make sure the fabric and ruler do not shift position.

4) Place ruler on fabric, aligning trimmed edge with appropriate measurement on ruler. Hold ruler firmly; cut as in steps 2 and 3. After cutting several strips, check fabric to be sure it is still on-grain, as in step 1.

Stitching Techniques

For pieced quilts, seam allowances are traditionally ¼" (6 mm); stitch accurate seam allowances, so all pieces will fit together exactly. If you have a seam guide on your sewing machine, check the placement of the ¼" (6 mm) mark by stitching on a scrap of fabric. If your machine does not have a seam guide, mark one on the bed of the machine with tape.

Use a stitch length of about 15 stitches per inch (2.5 cm). A shorter stitch length may be necessary for stitching curves and is used for securing stitches at the ends of seams. Adjust thread tensions evenly, so the fabric does not pucker when stitched.

Chainstitching is a timesaving technique for piecing. Seams are stitched without stopping and cutting the threads between them. After all the pieces are stitched together, the connecting threads are clipped and the seams are finger-pressed.

Although some quilters prefer working on one block at a time for the satisfaction of completing a block quickly, it is more efficient to sew an entire quilt top in units. Chainstitch together all the smallest pieces from all the blocks; then combine them to create larger units.

How to Chain and Assemble Pieces

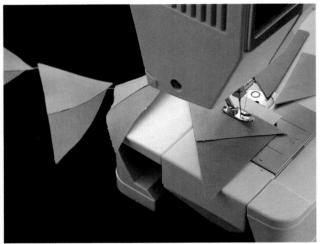

1) Start with smallest pieces; stitch together without backstitching or stopping between pieces, to make a chain of two-piece units. Clip threads between units; finger-press seams.

2) Add more pieces to units, if necessary for quilt block design, chainstitching them together. Clip threads and finger-press.

3) Chainstitch units together to create larger units. Clip threads and finger-press.

4) Stitch larger units together to form quilt block. Press with iron.

Pressing Techniques

Seams are usually pressed to one side in quilts; however, if you are planning to do stipple quilting (page 106) you may prefer to press the seams open to make it easier to quilt. When pressing seams to one side, it is best to press them to the darker fabric to prevent show-through.

Do not press seams with an iron until a unit or block has straight of grain on all four sides. Always remove all markings from the fabrics before pressing, because the heat from the iron may set marks permanently. When pressing seams, use steam rather than pressure, to prevent the layers from imprinting on the right side. A heavy pressing motion can distort the shape and size of the pieces. Press the blocks first from the wrong side; then press them again lightly from the right side.

The quilt should not be pressed after it is completed because pressing will flatten the batting.

Tips for Pressing

Finger-press individual seam allowances; pressing with an iron can distort bias seams. Press with iron only after a unit or block has straight of grain on all four sides.

Press long seams with iron by placing strips across, rather than lengthwise on, ironing board, to prevent distorting grainline as you press.

Sewing Designs with Squares

Many quilts are made from nine-patch quilt blocks. A Nine-patch block may be made from one-piece squares or pieced squares. A Double Nine-patch block alternates one-piece squares and checkerboard pieced squares. Each of the checkerboard squares is made from nine smaller squares.

There are two ways to assemble a nine-patch quilt block, the traditional method and the strip-piecing method. The traditional method works well when using larger pieces of fabric, such as 4½" (11.5 cm)

squares. The strip-piecing method is used primarily when making quilt blocks with intricate designs, because the piecing can be done quickly without handling small pieces of fabric. A double nine-patch quilt block may be assembled using both the strip-piecing and traditional methods.

The instructions for the Nine-patch quilt block (page 44) and the Double Nine-patch quilt block (page 45) make 12" (30.5 cm) finished blocks.

How to Cut Squares

1) Cut strips of fabric (page 39) the width of one side of square plus ½" (1.3 cm) for seam allowances. Stack three or four strips, matching edges exactly; place ruler on fabric near selvages at 90° angle to long edges of strips. Trim off selvages.

2) Place ruler on fabric, aligning short edge of fabric with appropriate measurement on ruler. Cut to same width as strips, holding ruler firmly.

How to Sew a Nine-patch Quilt Block Using Traditional Piecing

1) Cut five 4½" (11.5 cm) squares from Fabric A. Cut four 4½" (11.5 cm) squares from Fabric B.

2) Stitch one square of Fabric A and one square of Fabric B, right sides together, using ¼" (6 mm) seam allowances. Stitch another square of Fabric A to other side of Fabric B. Finger-press seam allowances toward darker fabric. Repeat to make two A-B-A units.

3) Stitch one square of Fabric A and one square of Fabric B, right sides together. Stitch another square of Fabric B to other side of Fabric A. Finger-press seam allowances toward darker fabric.

4) Stitch one A-B-A unit to the B-A-B unit, on long edges, right sides together; match seamlines and outside edges, keeping seam allowances toward darker fabric.

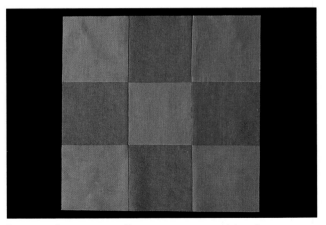

5) Stitch remaining A-B-A unit to the other long edge of B-A-B unit, as in step 4.

6) Press long seam allowances to one side; then press from right side.

How to Sew a Double Nine-patch Quilt Block Using Strip-piecing

1) Cut two scant 1⅞" (4.7 cm) strips from Fabric A and from Fabric B; cut strips in half to make four 22" (56 cm) strips. Cut four 4½" (11.5 cm) squares from Fabric B.

2) Stitch one B-A-B unit and one A-B-A unit, right sides together, using ¼" (6 mm) seam allowances. Press seam allowances toward darker fabric.

3) Trim short edge of each pieced unit at 90° angle. Cut ten scant 1⅞" (4.7 cm) strips from A-B-A unit. Cut five scant 1⅞" (4.7 cm) strips from B-A-B unit.

4) Stitch one A-B-A unit to one B-A-B unit on long edges, right sides together. Then stitch A-B-A unit to other long edge of B-A-B unit, right sides together, to form checkerboard.

5) Repeat step 4 for remaining checkerboard units. Press each seam toward side with two darker squares.

6) Stitch checkerboard units and plain units to form a nine-patch quilt block, as in steps 2 to 6, opposite.

Sewing Designs with Rectangles

Rectangles are used in many block designs. Strip-piecing methods are frequently used to piece designs created from rectangles. Streak O' Lightning is one of the easiest of all quilt blocks to strip-piece. Rail Fence uses the same piecing methods, but the strips are narrower.

Log Cabin is one of the most popular and variable traditional designs. Quick-cutting and quick-piecing methods can be used for the Log Cabin block.

Choose fabrics carefully for all three designs, as they define the overall pattern in the quilt top. For example, in the Streak O' Lightning design, choose a light color and a dark color. In the Rail Fence design, where two of the fabrics will define the zigzag pattern on the quilt top, light-to-dark color progressions can be effective.

For the Log Cabin design, three fabrics can be a light color and three a dark color; the center square should be a solid, contrasting, or complementary color.

The instructions for Streak O' Lightning and Rail Fence quilt blocks are used when only one quilt block is needed, such as in a sampler quilt or a pillow top. However, when making a quilt top from these designs, it is easier to sew an entire row of squares in a horizontal-vertical-horizontal arrangement the width of the quilt top and then join the rows together.

The instructions for the Streak O' Lightning quilt block (below), the Rail Fence quilt block (page 48), and the Log Cabin quilt block (page 49) make 12" (30.5 cm) finished blocks.

How to Make a Streak O' Lightning Quilt Block

1) Cut one 2½" (6.5 cm) strip (page 39) from each of two different fabrics. Stitch strips, right sides together, on long edge. Press seams to one side. Cut nine 4½" (11.5 cm) squares from unit at 90° angle to seams.

2) Stitch three squares together in a horizontal-vertical-horizontal sequence, as shown. Repeat with three more squares. Keep fabrics in same sequence, from left to right and from top to bottom, throughout quilt. Press seams to same side.

3) Stitch remaining three squares in a vertical-horizontal-vertical sequence. Press seams in opposite direction from other rows. Stitch rows together, with the vertical-horizontal-vertical row in middle. Press seams to one side.

How to Make a Rail Fence Quilt Block

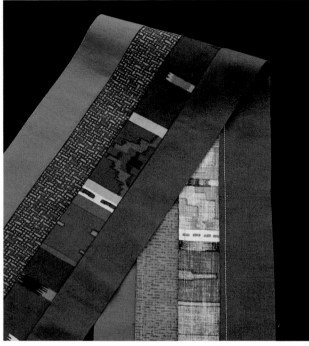

1) Cut one 2" (5 cm) strip (page 39) from each of four different fabrics. When strips are stitched together, outside strips define zigzag pattern. Stitch strips, in sequence, right sides together, along length. Press seam allowances to one side.

2) Cut four 6½" (16.3 cm) squares from unit, at 90° angle to seams. Stitch two squares together, in vertical-horizontal arrangement, as shown. Press seam allowances to one side.

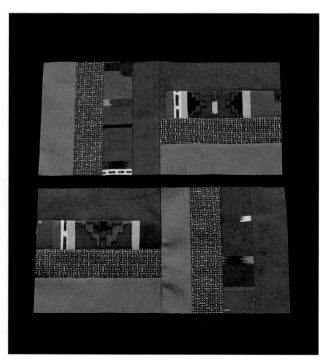

3) Stitch remaining two squares together in horizontal-vertical arrangement, as shown; keep fabrics in same sequence from left to right and from top to bottom throughout quilt. Press seam allowances in opposite direction from first row.

4) Stitch the two rows together, matching seamlines. Press seam allowances to one side.

How to Make a Log Cabin Quilt Block

1) Cut one scant 2¼" (6 cm) square from Fabric A. Cut one scant 2¼" (6 cm) strip (page 39) from each of six different fabrics. Label strips from B to G, as shown.

2) Place solid square on Strip B, right sides together. Stitch along one side. Trim strip even with square. Press seam allowance away from center square.

3) Place pieced unit on remaining length of Strip B, as shown. Stitch on long side. Trim strip even with bottom of pieced unit. Press seam allowance away from center square.

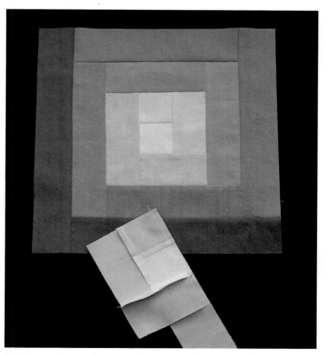

4) Place three-piece unit on Strip C at 90° angle to most recent seam. Stitch on long side. Trim strip even with bottom of pieced unit. Press seam allowance away from center square.

5) Place four-piece unit on remaining length of Strip C at 90° angle to most recent seam. Continue in this manner, stitching two strips of each color to pieced unit in sequence. Press seam allowances away from center square.

Sewing Designs with Triangles

Triangles are frequently used for quilt blocks. There are two methods for cutting and sewing triangles: the quick-cutting method with traditional piecing and the grid-piecing method.

The quick-cutting method allows you to cut several layers of fabric at one time. Some right triangles are cut with the grainline on the long side and some with the grainline on the short side. The grainline should be on the outside edges of each unit so the edges are stable and will not stretch when units are stitched together. The triangles are then assembled using a traditional piecing method.

The quick-cutting method is used to cut the right triangles for the Flying Geese quilt block (pages 52

and 53); avoid using a fabric with a one-way design. Flying Geese strips may be used for sashing or borders, or sewn together to make an entire quilt, as in the crib quilt, opposite.

The grid-piecing method (page 54) allows you to cut and piece the triangles in one operation. It is used whenever two triangles are stitched together to make a square, commonly referred to as a *triangle-square*, as in the Pinwheel quilt block (page 55). The grid-piecing method is especially useful when piecing small triangles.

The following instructions for the Flying Geese quilt block (pages 52 and 53) and the Pinwheel quilt block (page 55) make 12" (30.5 cm) finished blocks.

How to Cut Right Triangles Using the Quick-cutting Method

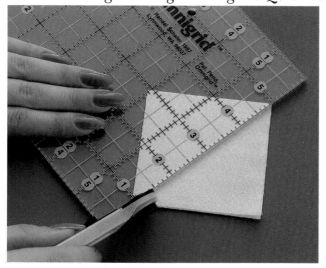

Triangles with short sides on grainline. Cut squares (page 43) with sides the length of finished *short* side of triangle plus 7/8" (2.2 cm). Cut half as many squares as number of triangles needed. Stack three or four squares, matching edges exactly. Place ruler diagonally across stack, holding ruler firmly; cut.

Triangles with long side on grainline. Cut squares (page 43) with sides the length of finished *long* side of triangle plus 1¼" (3.2 cm). Cut one-fourth as many squares as number of triangles needed. Place ruler diagonally across stack, holding ruler firmly; cut. Place ruler diagonally across stack in other direction; cut.

How to Make a Flying Geese Quilt Block

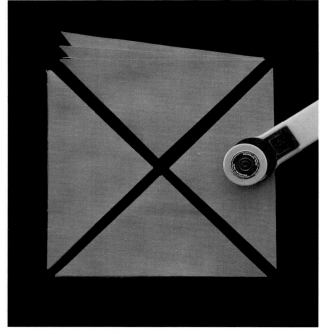

1) Cut three 5¼" (13.1 cm) squares of one fabric. Cut through squares diagonally in both directions so long side of each large triangle is on grainline.

2) Cut twelve 2⅞" (7.2 cm) squares of second fabric. Cut through squares diagonally in one direction so short sides of each small triangle are on grainline. Cut three 1⅞" × 12½" (4.7 × 31.8 cm) strips of third fabric.

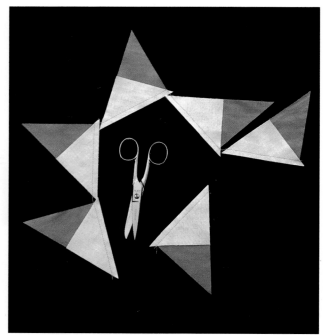

3) Stitch long side of one small triangle to short side of one large triangle, right sides together, using ¼" (6 mm) seam allowances and matching corners at base of large triangle; take care not to stretch bias edges. Repeat, using chainstitching, for remaining units; clip apart.

4) Finger-press seam allowances toward small triangle. Stitch a small triangle to other short side of large triangle, right sides together, matching corners at base of large triangle. Take care not to stitch a tuck in first seam. Repeat, using chainstitching, for remaining units; clip apart.

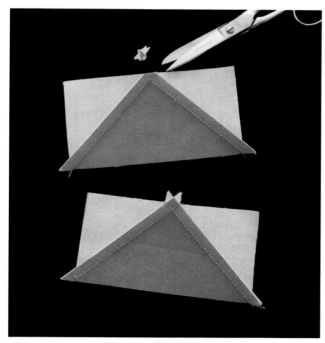

5) Press seam allowances toward small triangles. Trim points.

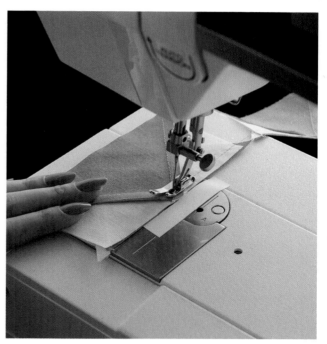

6) Place two units right sides together, matching top of one unit to bottom of other, so large triangles are pointing in same direction. Stitch, with point of large triangle on top, to make sure stitching goes through point. Repeat, using chainstitching, for remaining units; clip apart.

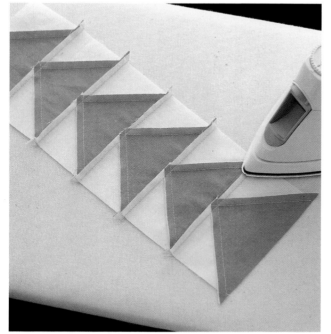

7) Stitch three units together to make a pieced strip of six units. Repeat for a second pieced strip. Press seam allowances toward bases of large triangles.

8) Stitch one long strip between two pieced strips; stitch remaining long strips at sides of block. Press seam allowances toward long strips.

How to Make Triangle-squares Using the Grid-piecing Method

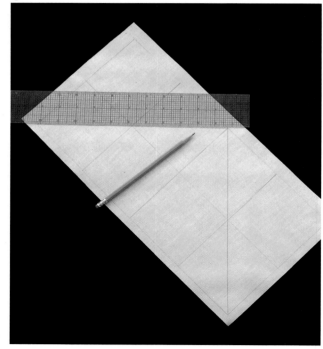

1) Cut one rectangle from each of two different fabrics. Draw grid of squares on wrong side of lighter-colored fabric, making grid squares ⅞" (2.2 cm) larger than finished triangle-square; each square of grid makes two triangle-squares.

2) Draw diagonal lines through the grid, as shown.

3) Draw diagonal lines through the grid in opposite direction.

4) Mark dotted stitching lines ¼" (6 mm) on both sides of all diagonal lines. Pin the fabrics, right sides together.

5) Stitch on dotted lines. Cut on all solid lines to make triangle-squares. Press seam allowances toward darker fabric. Trim points.

How to Make a Pinwheel Quilt Block

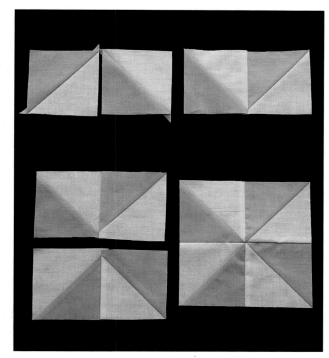

1) Cut one 7¾" × 15½" (20 × 40 cm) rectangle from each of two different fabrics. Draw 3⅞" (9.7 cm) grid, as in step 1, opposite. Draw the diagonal lines, stitch, and cut as in steps 2 to 5, opposite, to make 16 triangle-squares.

2) Stitch two triangle-squares, right sides together, as shown. Repeat with two more triangle-squares. Press seam allowances toward lighter fabric. Stitch two units together to form pinwheel, matching points. Keep seam allowances in alternating directions to eliminate bulk at points. Repeat for three more pinwheels.

3) Stitch two pinwheels together. Repeat with two remaining pinwheels. Press seam allowances in alternating directions.

4) Stitch remaining seam to form block. Press seam allowances to one side. Release stitching at centers of pinwheels to make seam allowances lie flat, if necessary, as on page 59, step 10.

Sewing Designs with Diamonds

Diamonds are frequently used to make star designs. Select fabric that has an all-over print or is a solid color rather than fabric with a one-way design or stripes, so you do not have to be concerned about the direction of the design when stitching the pieces together.

Cut diamonds carefully to ensure that the angles are accurate. The cutting directions, opposite, are for diamonds that have 45° angles. Other diamond shapes used in quilting require templates for accurate cutting. Because diamonds are cut on the bias, take care not to stretch the edges when stitching.

The instructions for the Eight-pointed Star quilt block (opposite) make a 12" (30.5 cm) finished block.

How to Cut Diamonds

1) Cut strips (page 39) the width of finished diamond plus ½" (1.3 cm). Stack three or four strips, matching edges exactly. Place on cutting mat, along grid line.

2) Place ruler at 45° angle to long edge of fabric; hold ruler firmly, and cut.

3) Shift ruler on fabric, aligning fabric edge with measurement mark that is equal to width of strip; hold firmly, and cut. Check accuracy of angle frequently.

How to Make an Eight-pointed Star Quilt Block

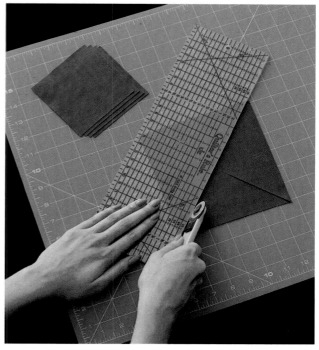

1) Cut eight 3" (7.5 cm) diamonds from one 3" (7.5 cm) strip of fabric, above, for star.

2) Cut four 4" (10 cm) squares and one 6¼" (15.7 cm) square of background fabric. Cut large square in half diagonally; then cut diagonally in other direction, to make four right triangles.

(Continued on next page)

How to Make an Eight-pointed Star Quilt Block (continued)

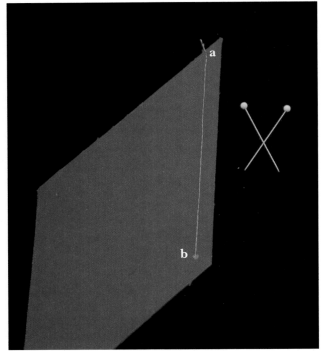

3) Mark wrong side of quilt pieces where ¼" (6 mm) seams will intersect, placing dots at right-angle corner of each triangle, both wide-angle corners of each diamond, and one corner of each square.

4) Align two diamonds along one side, right sides together, matching inner points **(a)** and dots **(b)**. Stitch from inner point exactly to dot; backstitch. Repeat for remaining diamonds.

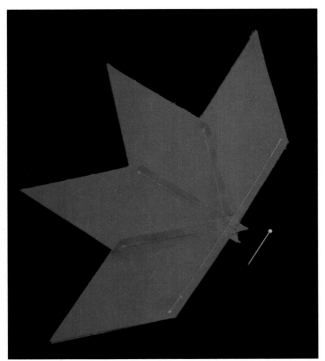

5) Stitch two 2-diamond units, right sides together, as in step 4, folding seam allowances in opposite directions (arrow). Repeat for remaining units.

6) Place two 4-diamond units right sides together. Pin, matching inner points at center. Fold seam allowances of each four-diamond unit in opposite directions to minimize bulk; stitch between dots, securing seams at ends. Do not press.

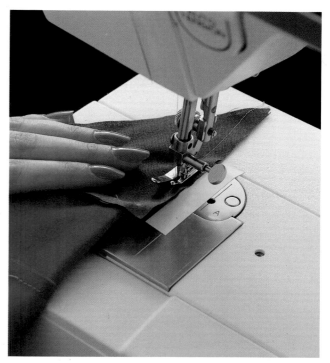

7) Align short side of triangle to a diamond, right sides together, matching edges at outer point (**a**) and dots at inner point (**b**). Stitch from outer edge exactly to dot, *with diamond side up*; backstitch.

8) Align remaining side of triangle to adjoining diamond, and stitch seam as in step 7, *with triangle side up*. Repeat for remaining triangles, stitching them between every other set of points on the star.

9) Align squares to diamonds between remaining points of star, matching edges at outer point (**a**) and dots at inner point (**b**); stitch *with diamond side up*, as in step 7. Align the remaining sides of squares and diamonds, stitching *with square side up*.

10) Release stitching within seam allowances at center of star, so seam allowances will lie flat. Press from wrong side, working from center out.

Sewing Designs with Curves

Some traditional quilt designs are based on curved pieces. Curves are the most difficult shapes to piece, but the more gradual the curve, the easier it is to piece. More intricate curved designs are usually done with appliqué.

Templates are required for cutting curved designs. They are available at quilting stores and by mail order, or you can make your own templates by cutting them from heavy cardboard or plastic template materials. Templates for machine-pieced designs include ¼" (6 mm) seam allowances. Make sure, when tracing and cutting templates, that the edges are smooth and the sizes are exact.

The Drunkard's Path is an easy curved pattern to piece. The pieced squares of the Drunkard's Path can be arranged in many different ways. Three different arrangements are shown, opposite. The method for cutting the templates and fabric for the Drunkard's Path can be used for cutting any machine-pieced curved designs.

The instructions for the Drunkard's Path quilt block (pages 62 and 63) make a 12" (30.5 cm) finished block.

Pattern for Drunkard's Path Template

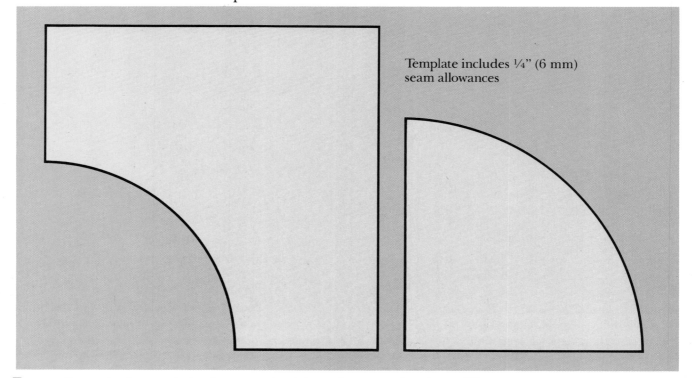

Template includes ¼" (6 mm) seam allowances

Trace pattern actual size onto tracing paper to make and cut template (page 62).

How to Cut Templates and Fabric for a Drunkard's Path Quilt Block

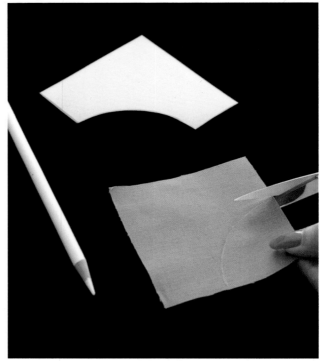

1) Trace template pattern (page 60) accurately onto tracing paper; cut. Place on cardboard or template plastic; trace. Cut accurately.

2) Place template on fabric; trace. Cut fabric on marked line, using scissors or rotary cutter.

How to Make a Drunkard's Path Quilt Block

1) Cut eight 3½" (9 cm) squares and eight 2½" (6.5 cm) squares from each of two fabrics.

2) Place large template on one large square, matching edges exactly; trace curve. Repeat for remaining large squares. Cut on marked lines. Discard scraps. Repeat for small squares, using small template.

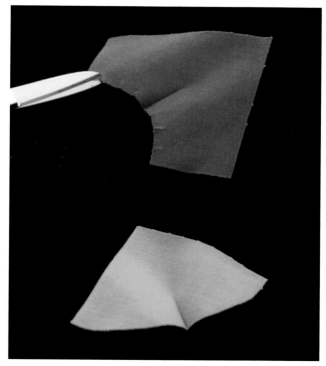

3) Fold each piece in half; finger-press to mark midpoint of curved edge. Clip seam allowances along curves of large pieces ⅜" (1 cm) apart, and a scant ¼" (6 mm) deep.

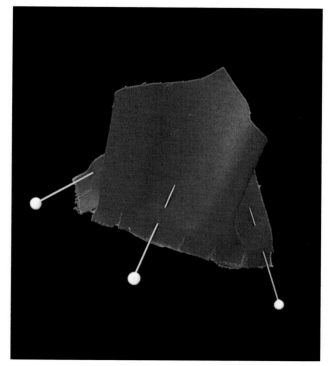

4) Pin one large and one small piece of different fabrics, right sides together, matching center creases. Pin at each corner, aligning edges.

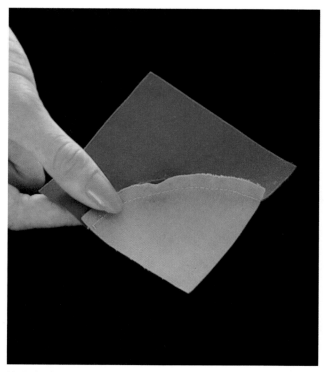

5) Stitch, with large piece on top, lining up raw edges as you sew. Finger-press seam allowance toward large piece. Repeat for remaining pieces.

6) Arrange pieced squares in block, four across by four down. First, stitch squares into rows of four; then stitch rows together to complete block. Press.

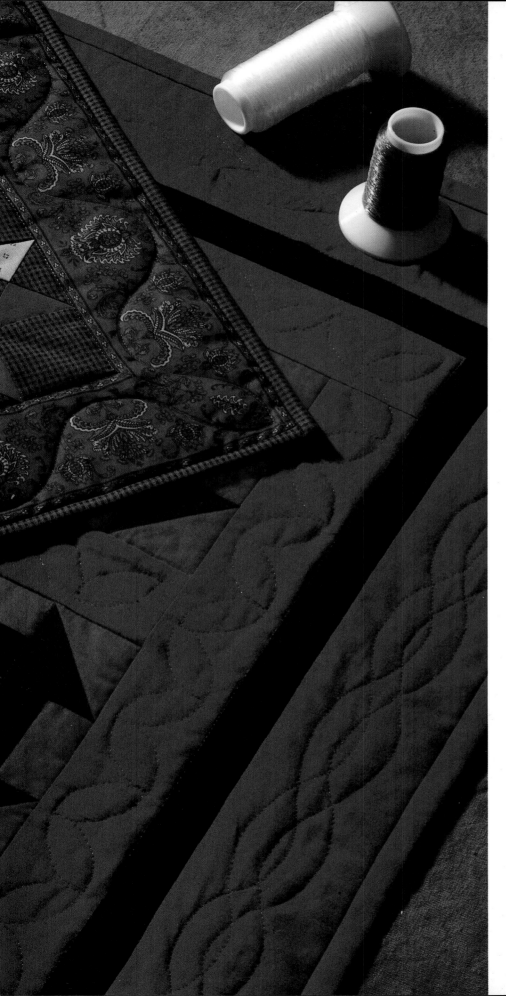

Sashing & Borders

Sashing separates the blocks in a quilt design, and borders frame the quilt. Both should be chosen carefully.

The sashing strips may be placed horizontally and vertically, or they may be placed diagonally. Once the blocks are completed, you may want to experiment with various widths of sashing. Sashing may be made from contrasting or background fabric and may be solid or pieced.

Make the final decision on a border design after the blocks and sashing are stitched together. A simple design that works well is a narrow, dark border next to the blocks, with a wide, lighter border around the outside. This sets off the piecing and unifies the quilt top.

Sashing

Sashing strips separate and frame individual quilt blocks, while they unify a quilt and change its finished size. A quilt top can be made larger by using sashing strips.

a

b

Plain sashing **(a)** is a good choice for a quilt with a complex block design and may be used with a matching border. Short, vertical sashing strips join the blocks into rows, and long, horizontal sashing strips join the rows. Sashing with connecting squares **(b)** adds more interest to a quilt. When this method is used, an outer sashing frames the blocks.

The sashing strips are cut after the quilt blocks are pieced and measured; this allows for any variance in size that may have occurred in seaming. Sashing strips are usually cut on the crosswise grain. If it is necessary to piece long sashing strips, the seam placement is usually planned so the seams are at the center of each strip.

To determine the number of sashing strips required, draw a sketch of the quilt top or arrange the quilt blocks on a large, flat surface. When estimating the yardage for sashing, do not include the selvages. Allow for some shrinkage if the fabric will be prewashed. On the cutting layouts, plan for about 40" (102 cm) of usable width for 45" (115 cm) fabric.

How to Estimate Yardage for Sashing

1) Draw a sketch of the quilt top, labeled with the measurements of blocks, borders, and sashing strips; draw seams for sashing on sketch.

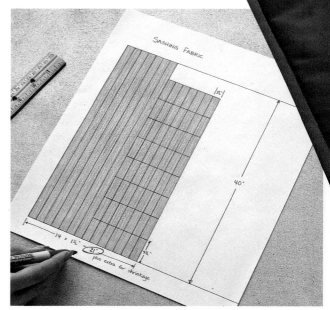

2) Draw cutting layout for sashing strips, labeling usable width of fabric. Sketch sashing strips, including seam allowances, on crosswise or lengthwise grainline, labeling measurements. Add the measurements to estimate yardage.

How to Make and Apply Plain Sashing

1) **Cut** sashing strips to the desired width of sashing plus ½" (1.3 cm) for seam allowances.

2) **Measure** sides of several quilt blocks to determine the shortest measurement; cut short sashing strips to this length.

3) **Stitch** short sashing strips between blocks, right sides together, to form rows; do not stitch strips to ends of rows. Press seam allowances toward sashing.

4) **Measure** length of rows to determine the shortest measurement. Cut the long sashing strips to this length, piecing as necessary.

5) **Mark** centers of sashing strips and rows. Place one long sashing strip along bottom of one row, right sides together; match and pin centers and ends. Pin along length, easing in any excess fullness; stitch. Repeat for remaining rows, except for bottom row. Press seam allowances toward sashing strips.

6) **Align** rows of blocks and mark sashing strips, as shown. Pin bottom of sashing strip to top of next row, right sides together; align marks to seamlines. Stitch as in step 5. Press seam allowances toward sashing. Continue until all rows are joined.

How to Make and Apply Sashing with Connecting Squares

1) Cut strips to desired width of the sashing plus ½" (1.3 cm) for seam allowances. From contrasting fabric, cut connecting squares for corners, with sides of squares equal to cut width of sashing strips.

2) Measure sides of several blocks to determine shortest measurement; cut sashing strips to this length. Stitch strips between blocks, right sides together, to form rows; ease in fullness. Stitch strips to ends of rows. Press seam allowances toward strips.

3) Stitch the remaining sashing strips alternately to connecting squares, to equal the length of the block-and-sashing row; there will be a connecting square at each end. Press seam allowances toward sashing strips.

4) Place one sashing unit along the bottom of the first block-and-sashing row, right sides together, matching seams. Pin along length, easing in any fullness; stitch. Repeat for remaining rows.

5) Pin bottom of one sashing unit to top of next row, matching seams, as in step 4; stitch. Press seam allowances toward sashing strip. Continue until all rows are joined. Stitch sashing unit to upper edge.

Frame Sashing

Frame sashing is pieced to form a unique design of parallelograms and triangles. For easy construction, the sashing pieces are stitched to each quilt block. When the framed blocks are stitched together, the sashing forms an eight-pointed star where the corners of four blocks meet, and the pieced triangles form squares in the design.

The unpieced quilt blocks, cut from a single fabric, may be embellished with quilting or appliqués. The sashing is constructed from gradations of a color. The choice of color in the sashing can create either a subtle frame around each block or a bold design.

The instructions that follow are for a bed quilt. For a twin-size, which measures about 68" × 86" (173 × 218.5 cm), three rows of two blocks are pieced. For a full/queen-size, which measures about 86" (218.5 cm) square, three rows of three blocks are pieced. The sashing is constructed around 12" (30.5 cm) quilt blocks. Each block framed with

3" (7.5 cm) sashing measures 18" (46 cm) square. Wide 16" (40.5 cm) borders complete the quilt and provide a background for decorative quilting. To eliminate the need for piecing, the border strips are cut on the lengthwise grain.

Cut two 3½" (9 cm) strips of each of the eight solid-colored fabrics for sashing; these will be cut into parallelograms (page 72).

Cut the four fabrics for sashing triangles into 7¼" (18.7 cm) squares; for a twin-size quilt, cut two squares of each fabric, and for a full/queen-size quilt, cut three squares of each fabric. Cut all squares diagonally in both directions (page 179, step 2), making four triangles from each square.

For the quilt blocks, cut 12½" (31.8 cm) fabric strips; cut the strips into squares, cutting six for a twin-size quilt and nine for a full/queen-size.

YOU WILL NEED

For twin-size:

¾ yd. (0.7 m) fabric, to be used for quilt blocks.

¼ yd. (0.25 m) each of eight solid-colored fabrics for sashing parallelograms; choose eight shades of one color.

Scraps or ¼ yd. (0.25 m) each of four fabrics for sashing triangles.

3¾ yd. (3.45 m) fabric, to be used for continuous-length 16" (40.5 cm) borders.

2¾ yd. (2.55 m) fabric in 90" (229 cm) width, or 5¼ yd. (4.8 m) in 45" (115 cm) width, for backing.

¾ yd. (0.7 m) fabric for binding.

Batting, sized for twin-size quilt.

For full/queen-size:

1⅛ yd. (1.05 m) fabric, to be used for quilt blocks.

¼ yd. (0.25 m) each of eight solid-colored fabrics for sashing parallelograms; choose eight shades of one color.

Scraps or ¼ yd. (0.25 m) each of four fabrics for sashing triangles.

4¼ yd. (3.9 m) fabric, to be used for continuous-length 16" (40.5 cm) borders.

2¾ yd. (2.55 m) fabric in 108" (274.5 cm) width, or 7¾ yd. (7.1 m) in 45" (115 cm) width, for backing.

¾ yd. (0.7 m) fabric for binding.

Batting, sized for full/queen-size quilt.

How to Make a Quilt with Frame Sashing

1) **Cut** a 45° angle on one end of strip for sashing. Place 4¾" (12 cm) mark of ruler along angled cut; cut strip to make parallelogram.

2) **Continue** cutting parallelograms from fabric strips, cutting six of each fabric for twin-size or nine of each fabric for full/queen-size.

3) **Stitch** two parallelograms of different colors to short sides of one triangle, as shown; finger-press seam allowances toward parallelograms. Trim points that extend beyond sashing.

4) **Repeat** step 3 to make four pieced sashing strips for each quilt block; randomly use each parallelogram and triangle fabric once in each set.

5) **Stitch** short side of one pieced sashing strip to one side of quilt block; begin and end stitching ¼" (6 mm) from edges of block, backstitching at ends. Repeat for remaining sides of block.

6) **Fold** quilt block diagonally, right sides together, matching seamlines and edges of parallelograms.

7) Stitch corner seam, backstitching at inside corner; do not catch seam allowances in stitching. Repeat for remaining corners.

8) Repeat steps 5 to 7 for remaining blocks, varying color arrangement. Arrange blocks in rows.

9) Stitch blocks into rows, matching points; stitch rows together, finger-pressing seam allowances at corners in opposite directions. Press the quilt top, pressing seam allowances toward blocks.

10) Cut and attach border strips (pages 84 to 89), cutting strips on lengthwise grain; cut width of border strips is 16½" (41.8 cm). Mark quilting design on border and blocks (page 102).

11) Cut backing and batting about 4" (10 cm) larger than quilt top. Layer and baste quilt top, batting, and backing (pages 96 to 99).

12) Quilt (pages 100 to 108). Cut and apply binding (pages 112 and 113); cut width of binding is 2½" (6.5 cm).

Star Sashing

Sashing strips with connecting stars create a sashing design bold enough to be used with plain quilt blocks. Quick methods for cutting and piecing are used to construct the stars, making this an easy quilt project.

The instructions that follow are for a quilt made from thirty 5½" (14 cm) quilt blocks and 2¼" (6 cm) sashing. The finished quilt with a double lapped border measures about 45" × 53" (115 × 134.5 cm).

✄ Cutting Directions

Cut eight 2¾" (7 cm) strips from the fabric for the sashing strips, and cut the strips into forty-nine 6" (15 cm) rectangles. Cut two 2¾" (7 cm) strips from the fabric for the stars; cut into twenty 2¾" (7 cm) squares. Cut seven 1⅝" (4 cm) strips from the fabric for the stars; cut into 160 squares to be used for the points of the stars. For the quilt blocks, cut five 6" (15 cm) fabric strips; cut into 30 squares.

YOU WILL NEED

> **1 yd. (0.95 m) fabric** for quilt blocks.
>
> **⅞ yd. ((0.8 m) fabric** for sashing strips.
>
> **⅔ yd. (0.63 m) fabric** for stars and ½" (1.3 cm) inner border.
>
> **¾ yd. (0.7 m) fabric** for 3½" (9 cm) outer border.
>
> **½ yd. (0.5 m) fabric** for binding.
>
> **2¾ yd. (2.55 m) fabric** for backing.
>
> **Batting,** about 49" × 57" (125 × 144.5 cm).

How to Make a Quilt with Star Sashing

1) Place 1⅝" (4 cm) square in one corner of sashing strip, with right sides together and raw edges even. Stitch diagonally as shown.

2) Press square in half along stitched line, matching outer edges to sashing strip. Trim fabric at stitched corner, leaving ¼" (6 mm) seam allowance.

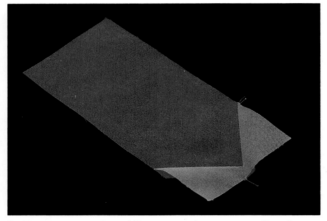

3) Repeat steps 1 and 2 at opposite corner. Continue piecing squares at one end of rectangles for a total of 18 pieced strips; these will be used as end strips.

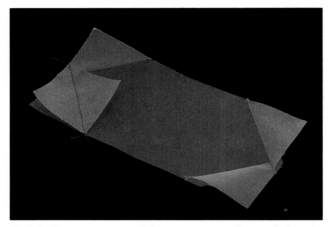

4) Stitch squares to all four corners of remaining sashing strips; these will be used as inner strips.

5) Stitch four end strips between five quilt blocks, placing plain ends at upper edge; this will be top row of quilt. Press seam allowances toward blocks.

6) Repeat step 5 to make a second row, placing plain ends at lower edge; this will be bottom row of quilt.

7) Stitch four inner strips between five quilt blocks to make one of the middle rows. Press seam allowances toward blocks. Repeat for three more rows.

8) Stitch five sashing strips alternately to the sashing squares, using an end strip at each end. Press seam allowances toward squares. Repeat for four more rows.

9) Pin one sashing unit along bottom of top row, right sides together, matching seams; stitch. Repeat for remaining rows, except for bottom row.

10) Pin bottom of one sashing unit to top of next row, matching seams; stitch. Continue until all rows are joined. Press seam allowances toward sashing.

11) Cut and attach border strips (pages 84 to 89); cut width of border strips is 1" (2.5 cm) for inner border and 4" (10 cm) for outer border. Cut backing 4" (10 cm) larger than quilt top. Layer and baste quilt top, batting, and backing (page 96).

12) Quilt (pages 100 to 108). Cut and apply binding (pages 112 and 113); cut width of binding is 2½" (6.5 cm). For wall hanging, apply fabric sleeve (page 165).

More Star Sashing Designs

Add variety to star sashing by piecing each star in a different color or by using a gradation of colors for the sashing strips. Or for a more intricate design, use strip-pieced sashing. When using a variety of fabrics, make a sketch of the quilt for easier cutting and assembly.

Graduated colors are used for the sashing strips in the quilt at right to add subtle interest to the design.

Bright stars in a rainbow of colors are used for this child's quilt. The multicolored printed fabric in the quilt blocks adds interest to the quilt. A brightly colored stripe is used for one of the fabrics in the triple border.

Calicos and plaids create a traditional look, with template-quilted blocks complementing the style. The sashing has been strip-pieced for a more intricate design.

Dark and jewel-tone fabrics create an Amish-style quilt. Strip-pieced sashing adds more interest.

How to Make Strip-pieced Star Sashing

1) Cut fabric strips on crosswise grain 1¼" (3.2 cm) wide, cutting three for each row of sashing. Stitch strips together lengthwise in desired sequence, right sides together. Press.

2) Cut pieced fabric into 6" (15 cm) rectangles for sashing strips. Make quilt as on pages 74 to 77.

Strip-pieced Sashing

Sashing with connecting squares gives a quilt an updated look when strip-pieced from graduated fabrics. Connecting squares in a bold contrasting color add another design element.

You may want to select a printed fabric for the quilt blocks and choose colors from that fabric to use for the gradation and connecting squares; the sharper the contrast, the bolder the design will be.

The instructions that follow are for a wall hanging made from nine 8" (20.5 cm) quilt blocks and 2" (5 cm) sashing. Random quilting lines complement the style of the quilt and create interest in the center of the quilt where the lines intersect. Instead of the

narrow binding that is usually used on small wall hangings, the traditional binding acts as a small border. The finished project measures about 32" (81.5 cm) square.

Cut 1½" (3.8 cm) strips from each graduated color for sashing strips; cut four strips of each color from fat quarters or two strips from 45" (115 cm) yardage. Cut one 2½" (6.5 cm) fabric strip from the fabric for the connecting squares; cut the strip into sixteen 2½" (6.5 cm) squares. For the quilt blocks, cut two 8½" (21.8 cm) fabric strips; cut into nine 8½" (21.8 cm) squares.

YOU WILL NEED

⅛ yd. (0.15 m) **each of eight fabrics,** or one packet of hand-dyed fabrics in fat quarters, for sashing.

⅛ yd. (0.15 m) **fabric** for connecting squares.

¾ yd. (0.7 m) **printed fabric** for quilt blocks.

⅓ yd. (0.32 m) **fabric** for binding.

1 yd. (0.95 m) **fabric** for backing.

Batting, about 36" (91.5 cm) square.

How to Make a Quilt with Graduated Sashing

1) Stitch one strip of each color together lengthwise, with right sides together and in graduated sequence; repeat for remaining strips. Press seam allowances in one direction.

2) Cut the pieced fabric crosswise into 2½" (6.5 cm) strips, using rotary cutter.

3) Stitch pieced strips between blocks, to form three rows of three blocks, with darkest color at bottom of quilt blocks; stitch pieced strips to ends of rows. Press seam allowances toward blocks.

4) Complete sashing, as on page 69, steps 3 to 5; arrange strips as shown.

5) Mark quilting lines (page 102); draw lines randomly across quilt top, drawing about four lines from each side. Layer and baste quilt top, batting, and backing fabric (pages 96 to 99). (Markings were exaggerated for clarity.)

6) Quilt along sashing as on page 105, using stitch-in-the-ditch method; then quilt on marked lines. Cut and apply binding (pages 112 and 113); cut width of binding is 2½" (6.5 cm). For wall hanging, attach fabric sleeve (page 165).

More Strip-pieced Sashing Designs

For more colorful designs, piece fabric strips from graduated blends of two or more colors. Or cut the connecting squares from several colors. To create more motion in the quilt design, vary the arrangement of the sashing strips.

Graduated strips are arranged in the quilt at right so the dark and light colors alternately radiate from connecting squares.

Printed fabrics in blended colors are used for the pieced sashing in the quilt at left. The blocks have been quilted, using free-motion quilting, to enhance the design of the mottled fabric.

Rainbow colors in the sashing are used with solid-colored blocks to make the quilt shown below. The blocks are embellished with template quilting.

Borders

A border frames the quilt and visually finishes the edges. The three basic styles of borders are lapped borders, borders with interrupted corners, and mitered borders. In general, a lapped border is used with solid fabrics or all-over prints, and a mitered border is used with striped or border-print fabrics. A border with interrupted corners is suitable with all types of fabrics.

Any of these basic styles can be used as a single or double border. A single border provides a simple frame for the quilt design. A double border can be used to enhance and unify a design by repeating two or more of the colors in the quilt top.

The border strips are cut after the quilt top is pieced and measured, because even the slightest variance in seam allowances can affect the finished size of the quilt top. The cut length of the border strips is determined by measuring through the middle of the quilt; this maintains the overall dimensions of the quilt.

Border strips are usually cut on the crosswise grain and pieced together for the necessary length. If seaming is required, the seam placement may be random; however, the seams should generally not be closer than 12" (30.5 cm) to a corner. For less noticeable seams, piece the strips diagonally. Borders cut from striped fabrics or border prints will usually have to be cut on the lengthwise grainline.

When estimating yardage, do not include selvages. Allow for shrinkage if the fabric will be prewashed; plan for about 40" (102 cm) of usable width on the cutting layouts for 45" (115 cm) fabric.

How to Estimate Yardage for Borders

1) Draw a sketch of the quilt top, labeled with measurements of blocks, borders, and sashing strips. Plan placement of border seams, if desired; draw seams on sketch.

2) Draw cutting layout for borders, labeling usable width of fabric. Sketch crosswise or lengthwise border strips, including the seam allowances; label the measurements. Add lengthwise measurements to estimate yardage.

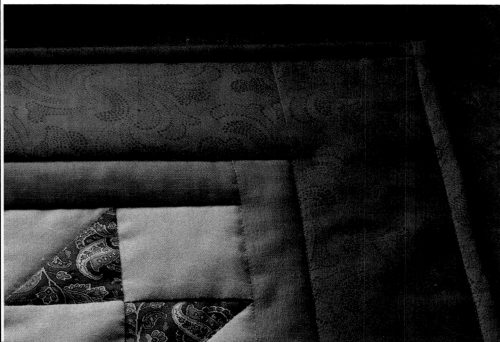

Single borders (above) include: lapped border (**a**), border with interrupted corners (**b**), and mitered border (**c**).

Double borders (left) may be lapped or mitered or have interrupted corners. The inner border is generally narrower than the outer border.

How to Make and Apply a Lapped Border

Single border. 1) Measure the quilt top across the middle. Cut two strips equal to this measurement, piecing as necessary; width of strips is equal to finished width of border plus ½" (1.3 cm).

2) Pin strip to upper edge of quilt top at center and ends, right sides together; pin along length, easing in any fullness. Stitch; press seam allowances toward border. Repeat at lower edge.

3) Measure quilt top down the middle, including border strips. Cut two strips as in step 1. Pin and stitch strips to sides of quilt top as in step 2. Press seam allowances toward border.

Double border. Apply inner border, following steps 1 to 3, above. Measure the quilt top across and down the middle, including the inner border; cut and apply the outer border as for inner border.

How to Make and Apply a Border with Interrupted Corners

Single border. 1) Measure the quilt top across the middle. Cut two strips equal to this measurement; width of strips is equal to finished width of border plus ½" (1.3 cm). Repeat, measuring the quilt top down the middle from top to bottom.

2) Cut four squares from contrasting fabric, with sides of squares equal to cut width of border strips. Stitch squares, right sides together, to ends of side border strips.

3) Pin upper border strip to upper edge of quilt top at center and ends, right sides together; pin along length, easing in any fullness. Stitch; press seam allowances toward border. Repeat at lower edge.

4) Pin and stitch pieced border strips to sides of quilt top as in step 3, matching seamlines at corners. Press seam allowances toward border.

Double border. Apply the inner border, following steps 1 to 4. Measure the quilt top across and down the middle, including the inner border; cut and apply outer border as for inner border.

How to Make and Apply a Mitered Border

Single border. 1) Measure quilt top across the middle. Cut two strips, with length equal to this measurement plus 2 times finished width of border plus 1" (2.5 cm); cut width is equal to finished width of border plus ½" (1.3 cm). Repeat for side strips, measuring quilt top down the middle from top to bottom.

2) Mark center of quilt top at upper and lower edges; mark center of upper and lower border strips. From each end of border strips, mark the finished width of the border plus ½" (1.3 cm). Place upper border strip on quilt top, right sides together, matching pin marks at center.

3) Match markings at ends of strip to edges of quilt top; pin. Pin along length, easing in any fullness. Stitch, beginning and ending ¼" (6 mm) from edges of quilt top; backstitch at ends. Repeat at lower edge.

4) Repeat steps 2 and 3 for sides of quilt top.

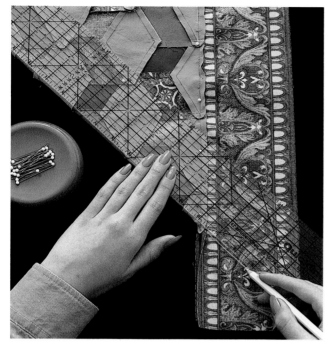

5) Fold quilt top at corner diagonally, right sides together, matching border seamlines; pin securely. Draw diagonal line on border strip, extending line formed by fold of quilt top.

6) Stitch on the marked line; do not catch the seam allowances in stitching. Trim ends of border strips to ¼" (6 mm) seam allowances.

7) Press seam allowances open at corner; press remaining seam allowances toward border strip. Repeat for remaining corners.

Double border. Apply inner border as in steps 1 to 7. Measure the quilt top across and down the middle, including the inner border; cut and apply outer border as for inner border.

Creative Borders

Borders, such as the appliquéd border shown here, can become an integral and important part of the quilt design instead of merely a frame for the quilt. Or borders can add an unexpected finishing touch, as shown on the quilts on pages 92 and 93.

Appliquéd Borders

An asymmetrical border, applied as an overlay, adds interest to a quilt. The edges of the border are appliquéd to the quilt top, following the design of the fabric. The border can provide a strong contrast to the pieced top or can blend subtly.

An appliquéd border may be added to as many sides of the quilt as desired. When planning the border, you may want to make a sketch of the quilt, or lay strips of the border fabric on the pieced quilt top to determine the desired size of the border pieces.

For the border, choose a printed fabric that can be cut and pressed along a design line. The yardage requirements will vary, depending on the size of the quilt and the width of the border strips. Estimate the yardage for the border as on page 84; for best results, plan for continuous border strips. When cutting the strips, you may want to allow extra width on the appliquéd borders to allow for adjusting the placement of the design line.

YOU WILL NEED

Printed fabric for appliquéd border, yardage determined as at right.
Fabric for narrow outer border, yardage determined as on page 84.
Pieced quilt top in desired quilt design.
Backing, yardage determined as on page 31.
Batting, about 4" (10 cm) larger than quilt top.

How to Apply an Appliquéd Border

1) Press quilt top. Determine side, or portion of side, to be covered by first border strip. Cut the length of border strip to this measurement; cut width is equal to desired depth at widest point plus ½" (1.3 cm). Mark inner edge of border strip along design line.

2) Stitch on the marked lines; trim ¼" (6 mm) from the stitching. Press under edge of fabric just beyond stitching line; clip as necessary.

3) Pin border strip to quilt top, making sure the edges overlap and the sides are parallel with the quilt. Blindstitch along pressed edges as on page 173, step 5. Trim excess fabric from wrong side, allowing ¼" (6 mm) seam allowance.

4) Measure adjacent side, or portion of that side, to be covered by second border strip. Cut the length of second strip to this measurement plus extra to overlap first strip; cut width is equal to desired depth at widest point plus ½" (1.3 cm). Mark inner edge of strip.

5) Stitch and press inner edge of second border strip as in step 2. Pin and blindstitch border as in step 3; trim excess fabric from wrong side, allowing ¼" (6 mm) seam allowance. Apply any remaining border strips as for second strip.

6) Cut and attach outer border, if desired (pages 84 to 89). Cut backing about 4" (10 cm) larger than quilt top. Layer and baste quilt top, batting, and backing (pages 96 to 99). Quilt (pages 100 to 108). Cut and apply binding (pages 112 and 113). For wall hanging, attach fabric sleeve (page 165).

Randomly pieced border adds a creative frame to this table runner with satin-stitched appliqués.

More Creative Border Designs

A creative border adds a new area of interest to a quilt, instead of a simple, complementary frame. The border can emphasize the colors used in piecing and can change the balance of the quilt.

Randomly pieced borders can incorporate fabrics that are too overpowering to use as continuous strips. Piece scraps together for the necessary yardage for the border strips.

Another way to incorporate several fabrics is by applying multiple borders. Instead of the usual single or double borders, several borders may be used on one quilt.

Unbalanced borders are especially pleasing on wall hangings. An unbalanced border creates motion in the quilt design, making the quilt more interesting when viewed from a distance.

Mitered border is applied to two sides only. The Pine Trees quilt (page 121) is displayed on point, with the top hanging free to reveal the quilt's patterned backing.

Bias tape is gently curved along the border of the contemporary crazy quilt (page 145) shown at left. Use the machine blindstitch to apply the bias tape (page 173, step 5).

Multiple borders of various colors and widths, shown below on a string-pieced quilt, were applied using the method for lapped borders (pages 84 to 86). The inner, or first, border is entirely red. The second and third borders are each half blue and half purple. The fourth partial border, applied only to the top and left side, repeats the red.

Contrasting insert strips make a contemporary frame for a landscape wall hanging; add the strips to the border. Start by applying the border strip on the left side of the quilt; then work counterclockwise, and miter the upper left corner.

Batting & Backing

Although batting is available in different sizes, it may need to be pieced for larger projects. Battings differ in loft and fiber content (pages 28 and 29). Loft is the thickness and springiness of a batting. It determines the degree of texture in a quilt.

The batting and backing should extend 2" to 4" (5 to 10 cm) beyond the edges of the quilt top on all sides, to allow for the shrinkage that occurs during quilting. It may be necessary to piece the batting and backing.

How to Piece Batting and Backing Fabric

Batting. 1) Overlap two pieces of batting, 1" to 2" (2.5 to 5 cm).

2) Cut with shears through both layers, down the center of overlapped section.

3) Remove trimmed edges. Butt batting edges, and whipstitch by hand to secure.

Backing. Cut selvages from fabric. Piece fabric as necessary, positioning seams as on page 31. Stitch, using a stitch length of 12 to 15 stitches per inch (2.5 cm) and ¼" (6 mm) seam allowances. Press seam allowances to one side or open.

Basting the Layers for Quilting

Basting keeps the three layers of the quilt from shifting during the quilting process. Traditionally, quilts were basted using needle and thread; however, safety-pin basting may be used instead. Lay the quilt out flat on a hard surface, such as the floor or a large table and baste the entire quilt. Or baste the quilt in sections on a table at least one-fourth the size of the quilt.

Press the quilt top and backing fabric flat before layering and basting. If basting with safety pins, use

1" (2.5 cm) rustproof steel pins. Steel pins glide through fabrics more easily than brass pins, and the 1" (2.5 cm) size is easier to handle.

If basting with thread, use white cotton thread and a large milliners or darning needle. Use a large running stitch, about 1" (2.5 cm) long. Pull the stitches snug so the layers will not shift. Backstitch at the ends to secure the stitching.

How to Baste a Quilt on a Surface Larger Than the Quilt

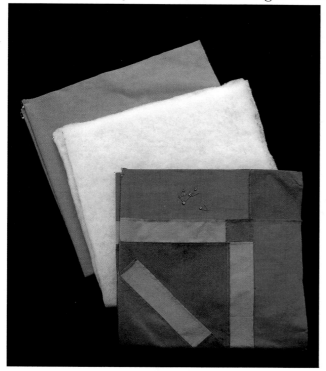

1) Fold quilt top, right sides together, into quarters, without creasing. Mark center of each side at raw edges with safety pins. Repeat for batting and backing, folding backing wrong sides together.

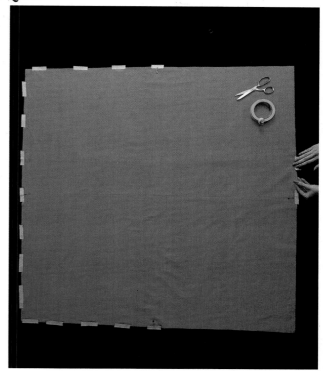

2) Unfold backing on work surface, wrong side up. Tape securely, beginning at center of each side and working toward corners, stretching fabric slightly. Backing should be taut, but not overly stretched.

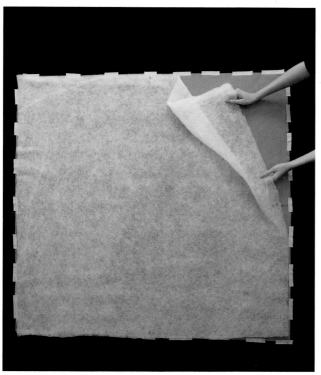

3) Place batting on backing, matching pins on each side. Smooth, but do not stretch, working from center of quilt out to sides.

4) Place quilt top, right side up, on batting, matching pins on each side; smooth, but do not stretch.

(Continued on next page)

5) Baste with pins or thread from center of quilt to pins on sides; if thread-basting, pull stitches snug so layers will not shift. Avoid basting on marked quilting lines or through seams.

6) Baste one quarter-section in parallel rows about 6" (15 cm) apart, working toward raw edges. If thread-basting, also baste quarter-section in parallel rows in opposite direction, as shown in step 2, opposite.

7) Repeat step 6 for remaining quarter-sections. Remove tape from backing.

8) Fold edges of backing over batting and edges of quilt top to prevent raw edges of fabric from raveling and batting from catching on needle and feed dogs during quilting. Pin-baste.

How to Baste a Quilt on a Surface Smaller Than the Quilt

1) Fold and mark quilt as in step 1, page 97. Lay backing on table, wrong side up; let sides hang over edge of table. Tape raw edges of backing to tabletop. Clamp backing securely to table, stretching slightly, beginning at center of each side and working toward corners; place clamps about 12" (30.5 cm) apart.

2) Place batting on backing, matching pins on each side. Place quilt top right side up on batting, matching pins on each side; smooth, but do not stretch. Baste one quarter-section of quilt as in steps 5 and 6, opposite. Remove tape and clamps.

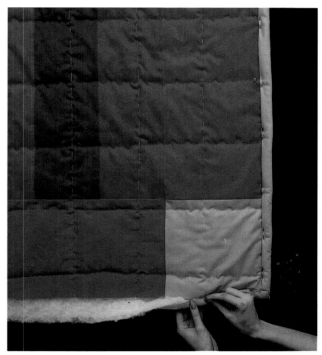

3) Move quilt to baste next quarter-section. Tape raw edges of backing to tabletop, stretching slightly; clamp all layers of quilt to edges of table. Baste quarter-section as in steps 5 and 6, opposite.

4) Repeat for remaining quarter-sections. Check for any tucks on backing; rebaste as necessary. Fold and pin-baste edges as in step 8, opposite.

Quilting Basics

Machine quilting is used to hold the layers of the quilt together, but it also adds surface texture and depth to the quilt. A large variety of quilting designs can be created using either machine-guided or free-motion quilting or a combination of both. Plan quilting designs to cover the quilt uniformly, because heavily quilted areas tend to shrink the fabric more than lightly quilted areas.

Machine-guided Quilting

In machine-guided quilting, the feed dogs and the presser foot guide the fabric. This method of quilting is used for stitching long, straight lines or slight curves, and includes stitch-in-the-ditch quilting and channel quilting.

Stitch-in-the-ditch quilting is used to give definition to the blocks, borders, and sashing. It is the easiest method of quilting, and is often the only type of quilting needed to complete a project.

Channel quilting is the stiching of parallel lines. The quilting lines may be either diagonal, vertical, or horizontal and are usually evenly spaced. Mark the quilting lines with a straightedge.

Free-motion Quilting

In free-motion quilting, the quilt top is guided by hand, allowing you to stitch in any direction without repositioning the quilt. The feed dogs are covered or dropped for this method of quilting. Free-motion

Channel Quilting **Stipple Quilting** **Motif Quilting**

quilting is used to quilt designs with sharp turns and intricate curves, and includes template quilting, motif quilting, and stipple quilting.

Template quilting is used to add designs, such as motifs and continuous border designs, to a quilt. Template quilting can be done using plastic stencils or tear-away stencils. For plastic stencils, designs are transferred to the quilt top (page 102). Tear-away stencils allow you to stitch the motifs without marking the quilt top. A design, printed on translucent paper, is pinned to the basted quilt top and torn away after quilting. Free-motion stitching is generally used for template quilting (page 106); however, some designs, such as cables with gentle curves, may be quilted using machine-guided stitching.

Motif quilting is used to emphasize the printed design of a fabric and is accomplished by outlining the desired motifs. Continue stitching from one motif to the next without stopping. Although free-motion is frequently used for this type of quilting, machine-guided quilting can be used if the motifs consist of subtle curves or if the quilted project is small and can be manipulated easily under the presser foot.

Stipple quilting is used to fill in the background. It can be used to create areas of textured fabric. For uniformity throughout a project, it is best to use loose stipple quilting when combining this method with other types of quilting.

Template Quilting   **Stitch-in-the-ditch Quilting**

Marking the Quilting Design

With some methods of quilting, it is necessary to mark the quilt before you begin. For channel quilting or template quilting with plastic stencils, mark the design on the quilt top before layering and basting, using a pencil or marking pencil intended for quilting. For stitch-in-the-ditch quilting, motif quilting, and stipple quilting, it is not necessary to mark the quilt top. For template quilting with tear-away stencils, the paper stencil is pinned to the quilt top after the quilt layers are basted together, eliminating the need for any additional marking.

If marking designs with pencils, test the pencils on a fabric scrap before using them on the quilt to be sure that the markings do not rub off too easily, but that they can be thoroughly brushed or erased away with a fabric eraser after quilting. Avoid using water-soluble marking pens, because the entire quilt must be rinsed thoroughly to completely remove the markings.

Marking tools and materials are helpful for marking intricate design lines. Marking tools and materials include plastic stencils (**a**), tear-away stencils (**b**), clear see-through ruler (**c**), and marking pencils (**d**).

How to Mark a Quilting Design

Marking pencil. 1) Press quilt top; place on hard surface, with corners squared and sides parallel. Tape securely, keeping quilt top smooth and taut.

2) Mark the quilting design, using straightedge or template as a guide, beginning at corners of quilt. Mark thin lines, using light pressure. For continuous designs, adjust length of several motifs slightly to achieve correct length.

Tear-away stencils. Press quilt top. Layer and baste quilt (pages 96 to 99). Cut stencil design, and place on quilt; secure with straight pins about 3" to 4" (7.5 to 10 cm) apart.

Quilt large projects by rolling one side of the quilt, allowing it to fit on the sewing machine bed. For even stitching, support the quilt to the left of and behind the machine.

Stitching & Handling

Cotton thread is traditionally used for quilting. Select the thread color according to how much you want the stitching to show. To avoid changing thread colors often, select one thread color that blends with all the fabrics in the quilt top. Or, to emphasize the quilting stitches and to add interest, select a contrasting or metallic thread for the quilting. Thread the machine, and loosen the needle thread tension, if necessary, so the bobbin thread does not show on the right side.

To maintain an even stitch length and to help the quilt feed through the machine evenly, do not allow the quilt to hang over the back or side of the sewing table. Set up the sewing area so the quilt will be supported both to the left of and behind the sewing machine.

Small projects are easily maneuvered as you machine-quilt. Before quilting larger projects, roll up one side of the quilt to allow it to fit on the sewing machine

bed. If the sewing surface is not large enough to hold the remaining width, roll up both sides of the quilt.

Plan the sequence of the quilting before you begin to stitch. Begin by anchoring the quilt horizontally and vertically by stitching in the ditch of a seamline near the center and then stitching along any borders; this prevents the layers from shifting. Next, stitch along any sashing strips or between blocks. Once the quilt has been anchored into sections, quilt the areas within the blocks and borders.

Stitch continuously, with as few starts and stops as possible. Prevent tucks from being stitched in the backing fabric by feeling through the layers of the quilt ahead of the sewing machine needle and continuously easing in any excess fabric before it reaches the needle. If a tuck does occur, release the stitches for 3" (7.5 cm) or more and restitch, easing in excess fabric.

103

Quilting Techniques

For machine-guided quilting, such as stitch-in-the-ditch and channel quilting, it is helpful to stitch with an Even Feed® foot, or walking foot, if one is available; this type of presser foot helps to prevent puckering. Position your hands on either side of the presser foot and hold the fabric taut to prevent the layers from shifting. Stitch, using a stitch length of 10 to 12 stitches per inch (2.5 cm), and ease any excess fabric under the foot as you stitch. The presser foot and feed dogs guide the quilt through the machine.

For free-motion quilting, such as template, motif, and stipple quilting, remove the regular presser foot and attach a darning foot. Set the machine for a straight stitch, and use a straight-stitch needle plate; cover the feed dogs, or lower them. It is not necessary to adjust the stitch length setting on the machine, because the stitch length is determined by a combination of the movement of the quilt and the speed of the needle. Use your hands to guide the fabric as you stitch, applying gentle tension. With the presser foot lifter in the lowered position, stitch, moving the fabric with wrist and hand movements. Maintain a steady rhythm and speed as you stitch, to keep the stitch length uniform. When changing your hand positions, stop stitching, with the needle down in the fabric.

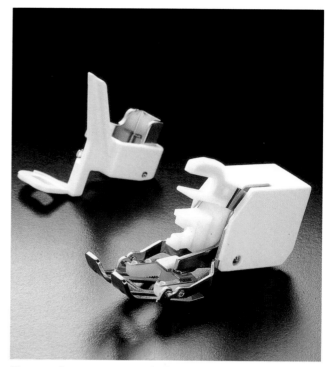

Presser feet recommended for quilting include the darning foot (left) and the Even-Feed or walking foot (right). An Even-Feed foot is used for machine-guided quilting. A darning foot is used for free-motion quilting.

Quilting techniques, including both free-motion and machine-guided, are used to add dimension to a quilt.

How to Secure the Thread Tails

1) Draw up the bobbin thread to the quilt top, by turning flywheel by hand and stopping with needle at highest position. Pull on needle thread to bring the bobbin thread up through the fabric.

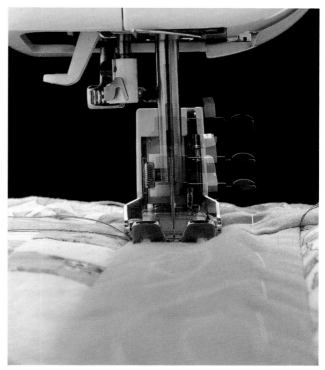

2) Stitch several short stitches to secure threads at the beginning of stitching line, gradually increasing stitch length for about ½" (1.3 cm), until it is desired length. Reverse procedure at end of stitching.

How to Quilt Using Machine-guided and Free-motion Techniques

Stitch-in-the-ditch quilting. Stitch over the seamline, stitching in the well of the seam.

Channel quilting. Stitch parallel quilting lines, starting with inner marked line and working outward.

(Continued on next page)

Single-motif template quilting with plastic stencils.
Mark design, using marking pencil and plastic stencil
(page 102). Stitch as much of design as possible in
long, continuous lines, without stopping.

**Continuous-motif template quilting with plastic
stencils.** Mark design, using marking pencil and stencil
(page 102). Stitch motifs along one side to points where
motifs connect **(a).** Or stitch one side of first motif,
then opposite side of second motif, and repeat **(b).**
Return to starting point; stitch motifs on opposite side.

**Template quilting with tear-away
stencils.** Stitch either single motif
or continuous motif, following the
directional arrows on paper stencil.
Tear away the paper stencil.

Stipple quilting. Stitch random,
curving lines, beginning and ending
at an edge and covering background
evenly. Work in small sections; keep
spaces between quilting lines close.
Do not cross over lines.

Motif quilting. Determine longest
continuous stitching line possible
around desired motif. Stitch around
motif without stopping; continue
to next motif. Stitch any additional
design lines as necessary.

How to Grid-quilt on the Diagonal

1) Tape quilt top to flat surface and mark quilting lines before basting quilt. Mark first line at an exact 45° angle to edge of design, starting at one corner; continue line to edge of design on opposite side.

2) Mark a line from end of previous line to opposite edge, keeping marked lines at 90° angles to each other and 45° angle to edge of design; continue marking lines in this manner until a line ends at a corner.

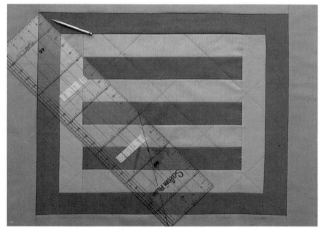

3) Mark a line, starting from another corner, if lines do not yet complete the grid design; continue marking lines to form a grid.

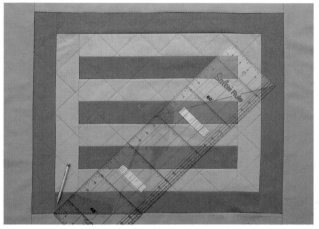

4) Mark additional quilting lines halfway between grid marks and parallel to previous lines, if smaller grid is desired.

5) Place quilt layers together and baste (pages 96 to 99). Stitch on marked lines, starting in one corner.

6) Stitch lines in same sequence as marked; turn fabric 90° at edge of design, pivoting with needle down.

107

How to Prepare a Large Quilt for Machine Quilting

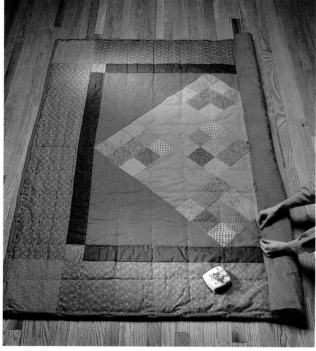

1) Lay the quilt flat, right side up. For quilts with polyester batting, roll one side to within 2" or 3" (5 or 7.5 cm) of center basting line. If necessary, secure roll with large safety pins or plastic headband. For quilts with cotton batting, loosely fold one side into accordion folds; it will stay without pins.

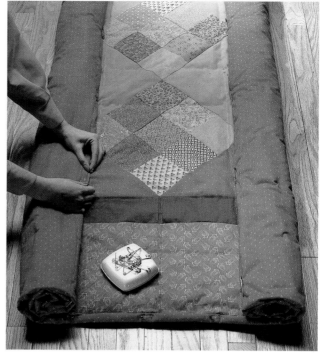

2) Roll or fold other side, as in step 1, if the sewing surface is not large enough to hold remaining width of quilt flat.

3) Fold quilt loosely along length, accordion-style, into lap-size bundle. Place bundle on your lap.

4) Pull quilt up from lap, section by section, so it is level with needle as you stitch. Do not allow quilt to hang over back or side of sewing table.

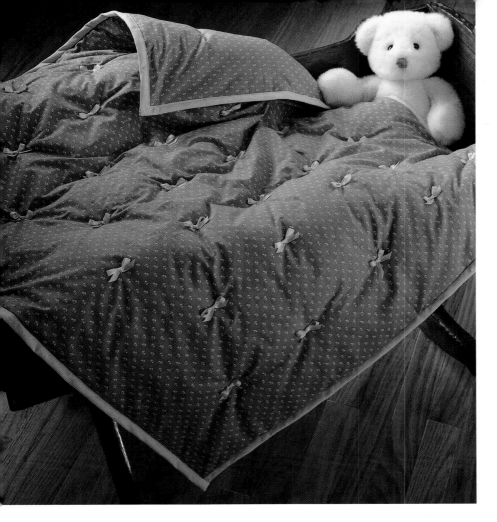

Machine-tying a Quilt

When using a high-loft batting, machine-tie the quilt to preserve the loft. A quilt can be machine-tied by using a zigzag or decorative stitch, or by attaching ribbons or yarns.

Mark the placement of the ties on the quilt top before basting it to the batting and backing. Stagger the rows of ties for greater interest and strength. Space the ties approximately 5" (12.5 cm) apart.

Three Ways to Tie a Quilt by Machine

Zigzag stitch. Adjust stitch length and width to 0. Holding threads behind needle, stitch several times through all layers. Adjust stitch width to a wide setting; stitch 8 to 10 times. Return stitch width to 0; stitch several times. Clip threads.

Decorative stitch. Use a decorative stitch instead of a zigzag stitch to secure quilt layers; adjust stitch length and width for an attractive design. Stitch in place at beginning and end of decorative stitch.

Ribbon or yarn. Cut one 3" to 6" (7.5 to 15 cm) length of ribbon for each tie. Tie into bow. Center bow over placement mark; stitch bow in place, using zigzag stitch, left.

Binding a Quilt

There are two methods for finishing the edges of a quilt. For mock binding (top), fold the backing fabric over the raw edges to the quilt top. For double binding (bottom), attach a separate strip of binding fabric.

Mock binding is an easy way to finish the edges of a quilt and makes use of the excess backing fabric needed during basting and quilting. Choose a backing fabric that coordinates with the quilt top.

Double binding is cut on the straight of grain and has two layers of fabric to provide a durable edge. The binding can either match or complement the quilt top.

The instructions for mock binding (below) and double binding (pages 112 and 113) make ½" (1.3 cm) bindings.

How to Bind a Quilt with Mock Binding

1) Machine-baste through all layers of the quilt, ⅛" (3 mm) from raw edges of quilt top.

2) Trim batting only, ¼" (6 mm) from edge of quilt top, ⅜" (1 cm) from basting stitches.

3) Trim backing 1" (2.5 cm) from cut edge of batting.

4) Fold backing diagonally at corner of batting; press foldline.

5) Fold backing so edge of backing meets edge of batting; press.

6) Fold backing over edge of batting and quilt top, covering stitching line; pin.

7) Cut out square of excess fabric at each corner. Pin corners.

8) Edgestitch along fold to secure. Remove basting stitches on quilt back. Slipstitch corners, if desired.

How to Bind a Quilt with Double Binding

1) Fold fabric in half on lengthwise grainline (page 39). Cut strips 3" (7.5 cm) on crosswise grainline.

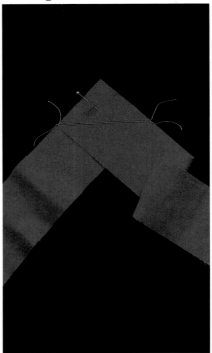

2) Pin strips, right sides together, at right angles; strips will form a "V." Stitch diagonally across strips.

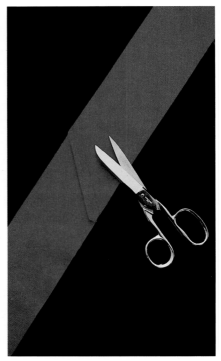

3) Trim the seam allowance to ¼" (6 mm). Press seam open. Trim points even with edges.

4) Measure one side of quilt; cut binding this length plus 2" (5 cm). Mark binding 1" (2.5 cm) in from each end; divide section between pins in quarters; pin-mark. Divide side of quilt in quarters; pin-mark.

5) Fold binding in half lengthwise, wrong sides together. Place binding on quilt top, matching raw edges and pin-marks; binding will extend 1" (2.5 cm) beyond quilt top at each end.

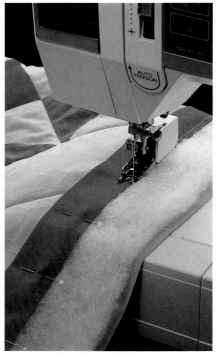

6) Stitch binding to quilt ¼" (6 mm) from raw edges of binding.

7) Cut excess batting and backing to ½" (1.3 cm) from stitching line.

8) Wrap binding around edge of quilt, covering stitching line on back of quilt; pin.

9) Stitch in the ditch on the right side of quilt, catching binding on back of quilt.

10) Repeat steps 4 to 9 for opposite side of quilt. Trim ends of binding even with edges of quilt top.

11) Repeat steps 4 to 7 for remaining two sides. Trim ends of binding to extend ½" (1.3 cm) beyond finished edges of quilt.

12) Fold binding down along the stitching line. Fold ½" (1.3 cm) end of binding over finished edge; press in place. Wrap binding around edge and stitch in the ditch as in steps 8 and 9. Slipstitch end by hand.

Cleaning Quilts

The care of a quilt depends on how it is used. If you are making a quilt to hang on the wall, it may only need to be vacuumed or shaken out occasionally. If you are making a quilt to be used on the bed, it will be laundered periodically. The less a quilt is handled, the longer it will last. Fabrics are easily damaged by abrasion and stress.

Dust and dirt abrade the fibers and shorten the life of a quilt. Quilts may be cleaned by vacuuming them, or by laundering them by machine or by hand. Dry cleaning is not recommended for washable fabrics, especially cottons; the chemicals used in dry cleaning may react with some dyes, resulting in color changes.

Vacuuming keeps quilts clean and minimizes the need to wash them. It is recommended that you lay the quilt on a flat, padded surface and vacuum it gently, using an upholstery brush and low suction. To protect the quilt from abrasion, you may place a fiberglass screen over the quilt and vacuum it through the screen.

Wash and dry quilts only when absolutely necessary, because washing and drying place stress on the fabric, particularly when done by machine. Before washing a quilt, test all dark and vivid fabrics for colorfastness (page 27).

Hand washing is gentler on the fabric, but quilts made of washable fabrics and battings may be washed and dried by machine. Whether you wash a quilt by hand or by machine, use a mild soap, without perfumes and other additives, such as dishwashing soap. Avoid soaps and detergents recommended for washing fine woolens; they may yellow cotton fabrics.

Thoroughly dissolve the soap and fill the machine or tub with lukewarm water before adding the quilt. Be sure there is enough water to cover the quilt, to help disperse any excess dye and aid in cleaning and rinsing. It is important to rinse all the soap out of the fabric; soap residue can coat the fibers, attracting dirt and discoloring the fabric.

Use extra care in handling a quilt while it is wet. Water adds weight, so, rather than pick up a wet quilt by a corner or edge, support the entire quilt in your arms or in a towel. Lay the quilt flat to air-dry instead of hanging it. Quilts may also be dried by machine. Machine drying fluffs the batting, but air drying is less abrasive to the fabric.

Tips for Washing and Drying Quilts

Machine Washing and Drying

Use large washing machine and high water level.

Wash on gentle or delicate cycle.

Remove quilt from washing machine immediately after washing, or wet fabrics may bleed.

Dry on cool to warm setting. Place dry terrycloth towel in dryer with quilt to shorten drying time.

Remove quilt from dryer before it is completely dry; spread flat on clean cloth, smoothing out wrinkles, to finish drying. Do not press.

Hand Washing and Drying

Use large tub, to keep quilt as flat as possible; for large quilts, use a bathtub.

Place quilt flat in tub, or in loose folds, as necessary.

Wash gently by hand, using a kneading motion; do not bunch, swirl, or twist.

Drain water, and refill tub with clear water; do not lift quilt. Repeat process until soap is rinsed out completely.

Press out remaining water, gently squeezing quilt against tub, working toward the drain. Blot with clean towels or mattress pad to remove excess water.

Lay quilt flat on clean sheets or mattress pad to dry. If drying quilt outdoors, avoid direct sunlight and cover quilt with clean sheet to protect it. If drying quilt indoors, use a fan to shorten drying time.

Storing Quilts

The best way to store a quilt is to keep it flat on a bed. Quilts usually suffer less damage from use than from storage. The most common forms of damage are fading, fabric deterioration, staining, and permanent creasing.

Fading of fabrics is caused primarily by exposure to light. Light also damages fabric over a period of time, making it brittle and weak.

Mold and mildew can cause staining, so quilts should be stored at a humidity of 45 to 50 percent. Staining and deterioration can also occur when quilts come in contact with storage materials such as paper and wood. As these materials age, they release chemicals that destroy fabrics. Acid-free papers and boxes are available for storing quilts.

Permanent creases are caused by folding and by pressure. When a quilt is folded for storage, the fibers along the folded edge are weakened and may break; the sharper the fold, the greater the damage. Putting weight on top of folded quilts increases the damage. Therefore, if you stack quilts in storage, refold and rotate the order occasionally.

Tips for Storing Quilts

Clean quilts thoroughly (page 115) before storing.

Store quilts in washed, unbleached muslin or cotton pillowcases or sheets. Acid-free tubes, tissue paper, or boxes may also be used; these may be obtained from archival storage mail-order sources or from some quilt stores.

Seal wood that will come in contact with quilts, using paint or polyurethane varnish.

Avoid exposing quilts to direct sunlight, to keep fabrics from fading and becoming brittle.

Avoid storing quilts in places where the humidity is high or where the temperature fluctuates greatly, such as attics or basements. Dry quilts thoroughly if they have become damp.

Do not store quilts in plastic bags.

Keep quilts away from direct heat sources, such as radiators, heat registers, or sunlight.

Pad folds of quilt with acid-free tissue paper or with washed, unbleached cotton fabric, to prevent sharp creases. Refold quilts every few months, changing the placement of fold lines.

Personalized Quilts

A quilt can be personalized in many ways. You can design a quilt around a subject of personal interest by making a commemorative, friendship, theme, or signature quilt. A memory quilt can be made for someone by using fabric from articles of clothing worn by that person from birth to adulthood. Or you can personalize a quilt by simply signing and dating it.

Signing and dating a quilt can be done during the piecing of the quilt by embroidering or machine-stitching the name and date in the corner block, or during the quilting by using freehand quilting. You can use a preprinted custom label or make your own label from fabric, using stitching or a permanent fine-line pen. The label can be sewn into the binding at a corner on the back of the quilt and then hand-stitched on the two remaining sides, or it can be attached completely by hand.

Friendship quilts have blocks designed and sewn by friends or family members. They are usually made to celebrate an occasion such as a wedding, an anniversary, or the birth of a child.

Theme quilts are designed around a central theme or idea, such as the outdoor theme, shown above, with pine trees, spider webs, and loons quilted into the blocks.

Signature quilts contain quilt blocks autographed by others, such as family members or the members of a church or community group.

Block-pieced Quilts

Pine Trees

The Pine Trees design is a popular motif for wall hangings. The blocks can be arranged in several ways for a variety of looks.

The grid-piecing method (page 122) is used to piece the *triangle-squares* in the Pine Trees quilt block, allowing you to cut and piece them in one easy operation; a triangle-square is two triangles stitched together on their longest sides to form a square. This grid-piecing method may be used for any quilt that has several triangle-squares.

For easier construction, the tree trunk and base at the corner of the quilt block is made from rectangles, then trimmed to the correct size after piecing.

The instructions that follow are for a wall hanging made from four 12" (30.5 cm) quilt blocks. The finished quilt measures about 24" (61 cm) square.

✂ Cutting Directions

Cut one 18" (46 cm) square from background fabric and one from tree fabric to be used for grid-pieced triangle-squares (**A**). Cut two 8⅞" (22.8 cm) squares from tree fabric; cut squares diagonally into triangles (**B**). Cut eight 2½" (6.5 cm) squares (**C**) and eight 4" × 5½" (10 × 14 cm) rectangles (**D**) from background fabric. Cut four 2" × 4" (5 × 10 cm) rectangles (**E**) and four 3" × 5" (7.5 × 12.5 cm) rectangles (**F**) from trunk fabric.

YOU WILL NEED

½ **yd. (0.5 m) fabric** for the top of the tree.

½ **yd. (0.5 m) fabric** for the background.

¼ **yd. (0.25 m) fabric** for the tree trunk.

¾ **yd. (0.7 m) fabric** for the backing.

⅜ **yd. (0.35 m) fabric** for the binding.

Batting, about 28" (71 cm) square.

Block Arrangements

Sawtooth effect is created by arranging the blocks with the tops of the trees toward the center of the quilt.

Starburst effect is created by arranging the blocks with the trunks of the trees toward the center of the quilt.

How to Make Triangle-squares Using the Grid-piecing Method

1) **Cut** one square or rectangle from each of two different fabrics. Draw grid of squares on wrong side of lighter-colored fabric, making the grid squares 7⁄8" (2.2 cm) larger than finished triangle-square; each square of grid makes two triangle-squares.

2) **Draw** diagonal lines through the grid as shown. Draw diagonal lines through grid in opposite direction as shown; there will be one diagonal line through each square.

3) **Mark** dotted stitching lines ¼" (6 mm) from both sides of all diagonal lines. Pin the fabric layers, right sides together.

4) **Stitch** on all dotted lines. Cut on all solid lines to make triangle-squares. Press seam allowances toward darker fabric. Trim points extending beyond edges of triangle-squares.

How to Make a Pine Trees Wall Hanging

1) **Make** 72 triangle-squares from 18" (46 cm) squares of fabric, following steps 1 to 4, above; in step 1, draw a grid of 2⅞" (7.2 cm) squares, six across and six down.

2) **Stitch** short sides of two 4" × 5½" (10 × 14 cm) rectangles cut from background fabric to long sides of 2" × 4" (5 × 10 cm) rectangle cut for tree trunk, with right sides together and raw edges even.

3) Stitch one long edge of 3" × 5" (7.5 × 12.5 cm) rectangle for tree base to one long edge of pieced rectangles, right sides together; match centers of rectangles. Press seam allowances toward tree base.

4) Stitch the large triangle cut from tree fabric to the opposite edge of the trunk unit, with right sides together and raw edges even. Trim the excess background and trunk fabrics to match the triangle. Press seam allowances toward darker fabric.

5) Stitch two rows of four triangle-squares as shown. Stitch rows together; attach to large triangle as shown.

6) Stitch two rows of triangle-squares and two background squares as shown. Stitch rows together; attach to opposite side of triangle, positioning background squares at top of tree.

7) Repeat steps 2 to 6 to make three more blocks. Arrange blocks as desired. Stitch blocks together to form two rows; stitch the rows together. Press quilt top.

8) Cut backing 28" (71 cm) square; press. Layer and baste quilt top, batting, and backing (pages 96 to 99).

9) Quilt (pages 100 to 108). Cut and apply binding (pages 112 and 113); cut width of binding is 2½" (6.5 cm). Attach fabric sleeve (page 165); to hang quilt on point, attach second sleeve to adjacent side.

More Pine Trees Designs

Corner triangles may be added to the sides of each tree in a Pine Trees quilt, as shown above, setting the trees vertically and making 17" (43 cm) quilt blocks. To cut the triangles for the corners, cut 9⅜" (24 cm) squares from four fabrics in half diagonally; one triangle of each color is used for each block.

The quilt above has 16 blocks, four across and four down. With a 4" (10 cm) border, the finished quilt measures about 76" (193 cm) square, a size suitable for a bed quilt.

The Pine Trees design is fun to make in seasonal colors. Make one with a Christmas theme, or change the colors for a spring, summer, fall, or winter quilt. Combine the seasonal blocks for a four-season quilt that can be displayed year-round.

Even though this design is called Pine Trees, it need not resemble trees at all. With the use of unexpected colors and a block arrangement that radiates out from the center, a four-block quilt can create a colorful starburst effect.

Seasonal theme (left) can be created by using different fabrics for each block. Sashing (pages 66 to 68) has been added to set the blocks apart, and a lapped border (pages 84 to 86) frames the quilt. To make the 18 triangle-squares necessary for each block, use the grid-piecing method on page 122, marking the 2⅞" (7.2 cm) grid, three across and three down, on 9" (23 cm) square of fabric.

Starburst effect (right) is created by the arrangement of the blocks and by using nontraditional colors. For the 16 triangle-squares of the inner rows, mark the 2⅞" (7.2 cm) grid, four across and four down, on 12" (30.5 cm) square of fabric. For the 20 triangle-squares of the outer rows, mark the 2⅞" (7.2 cm) grid, five across and four down, on 15" × 12" (38 × 30.5 cm) rectangle of fabric.

Holiday fabrics (left) can make a festive wall hanging for the Christmas season. A lapped border (pages 84 to 86) frames the quilt. The triangle-squares are grid-pieced as for the quilt with a starburst effect, above.

Bow Ties

Bow Ties is a versatile quilt design that lends itself to many block arrangements. The Bow Ties design is shown here in four different arrangements. In the traditional pattern (opposite), the blocks are arranged in rows, with each bow tie facing in the same direction. As shown in the quilts below, the blocks may also be turned alternately for a zigzag pattern, arranged in units of four blocks for an octagonal pattern, or arranged in a staggered pattern.

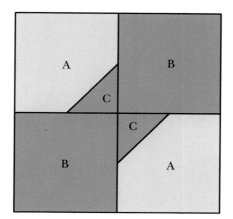

Traditionally, templates were used to make a Bow Ties quilt. But this design can now be made using a simplified method that enables quick cutting and chainstitching. The easy method for constructing a single Bow Ties block is on page 128. To make enough blocks for an entire quilt, construct them quickly and efficiently, using chainstitching (page 40).

The instructions that follow are for a wall hanging made from sixty-four 4" (10 cm) quilt blocks. The finished quilt measures about 37" (94 cm) square.

✂ Cutting Directions

Each block requires two 2½" (6.5 cm) squares (**A**) from background fabric and two 2½" (6.5 cm) squares (**B**) from bow-tie fabric, cut from 2½" (6.5 cm) fabric strips. Each block also requires two 1½" (3.8 cm) squares from bow-tie fabric, which will be pieced and trimmed to make triangles (**C**); cut the 1½" (3.8 cm) squares from 1½" (3.8 cm) fabric strips.

The Bow Ties project requires 16 blocks of each bow-tie color. Cut eight 2½" (6.5 cm) strips from background fabric, cutting each strip into squares to make 128 background squares. Cut two 2½" (6.5 cm) strips from each of four bow-tie fabrics, cutting each strip into squares to make 32 squares from each fabric. Cut two 1½" (3.8 cm) strips from each bow-tie fabric, cutting each strip to make 32 squares from each fabric.

YOU WILL NEED

⅜ yd. **(0.35 m) fabric** in each of four colors for bow ties.

¾ yd. **(0.7 m) fabric** for background.

¾ yd. **(0.7 m) fabric** for border and binding.

1¼ yd. **(1.15 m) fabric** for backing.

Batting, about 41" (104 cm) square.

Block Arrangements

Zigzag pattern has the quilt blocks turned in alternate directions.

Octagonal pattern is created by arranging the quilt blocks in units of four.

Staggered pattern of quilt blocks forms diagonal rows.

How to Make a Bow Ties Quilt Block

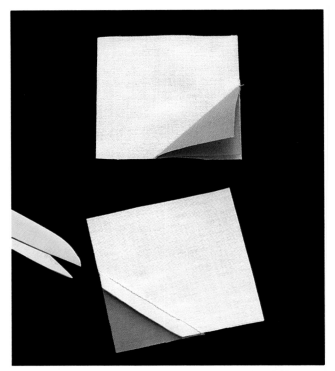

1) Place 1½" (3.8 cm) square in one corner of a background square, with right sides together and raw edges even. Stitch diagonally from corner to corner as shown. Repeat for a second pieced square.

2) Press small square in half along stitched line, matching outer edges to large square. Trim fabric at stitched corner, leaving ¼" (6 mm) seam allowance. Repeat for second pieced square.

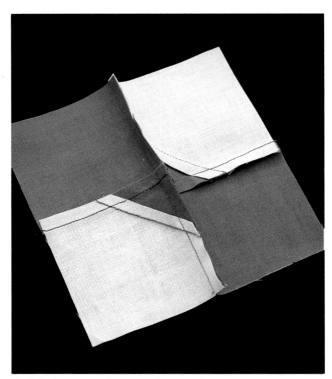

3) Stitch each pieced square to one square from bow-tie fabric, as shown, to make two half-block units.

4) Stitch two units together to form a bow tie, finger-pressing center seam allowances in opposite directions.

How to Make a Bow Ties Quilt

1) Piece blocks for each color, following steps 1 to 4, opposite; for staggered pattern (page 127), construct two half-block units of each color, following steps 1 to 3, opposite.

2) Arrange blocks, eight across and eight down, as shown in the quilts on pages 126 and 127. For staggered pattern, use half-block units to complete design.

3) Stitch the blocks into rows; stitch rows together, finger-pressing seam allowances in opposite directions. Press quilt top. Cut and attach border strips (pages 84 to 89); cut width of border strips is 3" (7.5 cm).

4) Cut backing 4" (10 cm) larger than quilt top; press. Layer and baste the quilt top, batting, and backing (pages 96 to 99).

5) Quilt (pages 100 to 108). Cut and apply binding (pages 112 and 113); cut width of binding is 2½" (6.5 cm). For wall hanging, attach fabric sleeve (page 165).

More Bow Ties Designs

The fabric and color selection can dramatically change the look of a Bow Ties quilt. Fabrics that resemble those used in men's neckties give an authentic look. Colors in the Amish tradition have a more striking effect, and subtle variations of gradated colors result in a more subdued quilt. Add variety to a Bow Ties quilt by choosing fabric scraps with different colors and textures for each block.

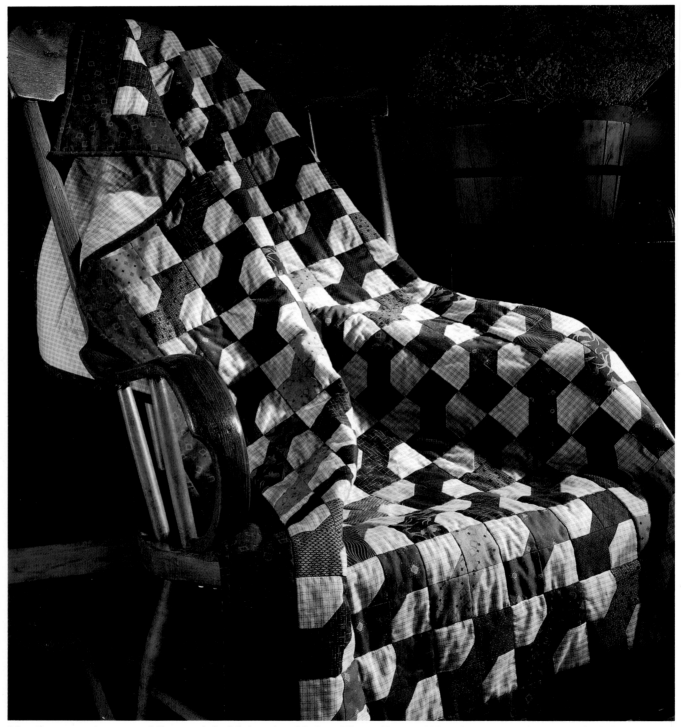

Many cotton prints resembling necktie fabrics give this Bow Ties quilt a traditional menswear look. An old-fashioned plaid fabric is used for the background of the quilt.

Amish colors used in the traditional pattern create a wall hanging with heirloom appeal. In the Amish tradition of intentionally making the quilt imperfect, one quilt block has been turned in the opposite direction, adding an interesting design element.

Gradations of warm colors are used to achieve a soft look. Make a sketch of the quilt to determine how many blocks of each color you will need.

Scraps can be used to create an eclectic look, with muslin used for the background squares. The octagonal pattern is interrupted with narrow sashing strips.

Houses

Pieced picture quilts depicting houses were first developed in the 1800s. They remain popular today because of the versatility of the design. This version of a traditional house block is also quick and easy to cut and piece.

By varying the use of color, you can create a nighttime effect, as shown opposite, using dark fabrics for the houses and sky, and yellow to illuminate the windows and doors. Or create a daytime effect, using bright colors for the houses and black for the windows and doors, as shown in the quilt on page 137.

The instructions that follow are for a wall hanging made from nine 8" (20.5 cm) quilt blocks. Sashing with interrupted corners frames the blocks and unifies the overall design. The finished quilt with a single lapped border measures about 36" (91.5 cm) square.

✂ Cutting Directions

Cut the correct number of pieces for each of nine quilt blocks, using the dimensions in the chart below. From each of the three house fabrics, cut enough house and gable pieces for three quilt blocks, making enough for a total of nine blocks.

Pieces to Cut for Each Quilt Block

	Pieces	Number and Size
House	A	One 1½" × 1¾" (3.8 × 4.5 cm) rectangle.
	B	Two 1⅞" × 4½" (4.7 × 11.5 cm) rectangles.
	C	One 1½" × 2½" (3.8 × 6.5 cm) rectangle.
	D	One 2½" (6.5 cm) square.
	E	Two 1½" × 4½" (3.8 × 11.5 cm) rectangles.
Gable	F	One 5¼" (13.2 cm) square, cut diagonally in both directions; use one triangle for each quilt block.
Door	G	One 1¾" × 3½" (4.5 × 9 cm) rectangle.
Window	H	One 1½" × 2½" (3.8 × 6.5 cm) rectangle.
Roof	I	One parallelogram (page 56), cut from 2½" (6.5 cm) strip.
Chimney	J	One 1½" (3.8 cm) square.
Sky	K	Two 1½" × 4" (3.8 × 10 cm) rectangles.
	L	One 2⅞" (7.2 cm) square, cut in half diagonally for two triangles.
Ground	M	One 1½" × 8½" (3.8 × 21.8 cm) rectangle.

YOU WILL NEED

⅜ yd. (0.35 m) fabric in each of three colors for houses and gables.

⅛ yd. (0.15 m) fabric for doors and windows.

⅛ yd. (0.15 m) fabric for roofs.

⅛ yd. (0.15 m) fabric or scraps in each color for chimneys, sky, and ground.

⅓ yd. (0.32 m) fabric for 1½" (3.8 cm) sashing.

½ yd. (0.5 m) fabric for 3" (7.5 cm) border.

⅓ yd. (0.32 m) fabric for binding.

1⅛ yd. (1.05 m) fabric for backing.

Batting, about 40" (102 cm) square.

How to Make a Houses Quilt

1) Cut 45° angle on one end of fabric strip for roof. Place 3¼" (8.2 cm) mark on ruler along angle-cut; cut strip to make parallelogram. Repeat for eight more roof pieces.

2) Stitch fabric strips for the sky to each side of the chimney piece.

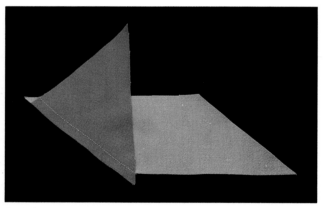

3) Stitch gable piece to roof piece as shown; use a gable color that will contrast with the house color. Finger-press seam allowance toward roof.

4) Stitch long edge of one sky triangle to one side of roof; stitch long edge of second sky triangle to gable. Finger-press seam allowances toward sky. Trim points extending beyond edges of unit.

5) Stitch 1½" × 1¾" (3.8 × 4.5 cm) rectangle of house fabric to top of door. Stitch one 1⅞" × 4½" (4.7 × 11.5 cm) rectangle of house fabric to each side of pieced door section as shown.

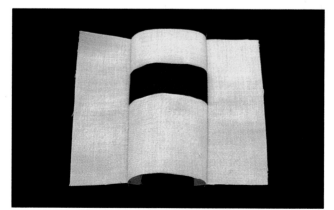

6) Stitch 1½" × 2½" (3.8 × 6.5 cm) rectangle of house fabric to the top of the window; stitch 2½" (6.5 cm) square to the bottom of the window. Stitch one 1½" × 4½" (3.8 × 11.5 cm) rectangle to each side of pieced window section.

7) Stitch pieced door section and pieced window section together. Stitch pieced strips and ground strip together. Press quilt block.

8) Repeat steps 2 to 7 for remaining quilt blocks. Arrange blocks in rows of three.

9) Cut sashing strips with connecting squares (page 69) and attach to the quilt blocks; you will need 24 sashing pieces with a cut width of 2" (5 cm) and sixteen 2" (5 cm) connecting squares.

10) Cut and attach border strips (pages 84 to 89); cut width of border strips is 3½" (9 cm).

11) Cut 40" (102 cm) square of backing fabric. Layer and baste quilt top, batting, and backing (pages 96 to 99).

12) Quilt, using stitch-in-the-ditch method (pages 104 and 105) around blocks, sashing, and borders; quilt houses as desired. Cut and apply binding (pages 112 and 113); cut width of binding is 2" (5 cm). For wall hanging, attach fabric sleeve (page 165). (Contrasting thread was used to show detail.)

More Houses Designs

Houses designs allow you to have fun experimenting with colors and textures. Select colors to suggest a mood or time of day. Or choose colors or fabrics to depict a particular type of house.

Bright crayon colors create a cheerful coverlet for a child's room. The twin-size bed quilt shown above consists of 48 quilt blocks, six blocks across and eight down. The finished size of the quilt including a 3½" (9 cm) border, is about 65½" × 85½" (166.8 × 217.3 cm).

Houses quilt blocks can be embellished with appliqués, embroidery, or decorative buttons to add landscaping or architectural details.

Daytime effect is created by using sunny colors for the houses and black for the doors and windows.

Embellished houses are decorated with lace, trims, beads, and buttons for a whimsical effect.

Ocean Waves

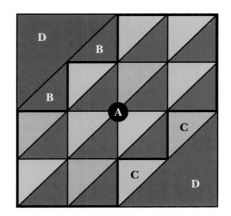

The Ocean Waves design is a traditional quilt design with rows of triangles that create a gentle flowing motion. Planning the color scheme for an Ocean Waves quilt can look difficult, but is actually simple to do.

The waves portion of an Ocean Waves block is made from ten triangle-squares plus four additional small triangles. Two large triangles in opposite corners complete the block. The grid-piecing method (page 122) is used to construct the triangle-squares. If you are unfamiliar with this type of construction, you may want to make the smaller Pine Trees project (page 121) before making the more challenging Ocean Waves project. The large triangles at the corners form the squares in the design when the blocks are stitched together.

For the quilt shown opposite, choose one dark-colored solid fabric, which will be used for one half of each triangle-square; repeating one fabric in each triangle-square gives the quilt a unified color scheme. Choose eight light-colored solid fabrics, which will be used for the remaining half of the triangle-squares. To minimize the appearance of the seams in the pieced squares, choose a printed fabric for the large triangles.

The instructions that follow are for a wall hanging or lap quilt made from twenty-four 8" (20.5 cm) quilt blocks. The finished quilt with a double lapped border measures about 40" × 56" (102 × 142 cm).

✂ Cutting Directions

For grid-pieced triangle-squares **(A),** cut eight 9½" × 15" (24.3 × 38 cm) rectangles from dark-colored solid fabric, and cut one 9½" × 15" (24.3 × 38 cm) rectangle from each of the eight light-colored solid fabrics.

Cut twenty-four 2⅞" (7.2 cm) squares from dark-colored solid fabric; cut squares in half diagonally to make 48 small triangles **(B).** Cut three 2⅞" (7.2 cm) squares from each of eight light-colored solid fabrics; cut squares in half diagonally to make 48 more small triangles **(C).** Cut twenty-four 4⅞" (12.2 cm) squares from printed fabric; cut squares in half diagonally to make 48 large triangles **(D).**

YOU WILL NEED

1⅛ **yd. (1.05 m) dark-colored solid fabric** for one half of each triangle-square.

⅓ **yd. (0.32 m) each of eight light-colored solid fabrics,** or eight fat quarters, for remaining halves of triangle-squares.

½ **yd. (0.5 m) printed fabric** for large triangles.

¼ **yd. (0.25 m) fabric** for 1" (2.5 cm) inner border.

⅔ **yd. (0.63 m) fabric** for 3" (7.5 cm) outer border.

½ **yd. (0.5 m) fabric** for binding.

2½ **yd. (2.3 m) fabric** for backing.

Batting, about 44" × 60" (112 × 152.5 cm).

How to Make an Ocean Waves Quilt

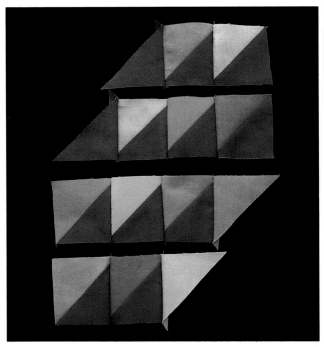

1) **Assemble** triangle-squares from 9½" × 15" (24.3 × 38 cm) rectangles, as on page 122, steps 1 to 4; in step 1, draw grids of 2⅞" (7.2 cm) squares, five across and three down. Make separate stacks of triangle-squares from each grid.

2) **Stitch** triangle-squares and small triangles into four rows as shown; use a triangle-square from each stack, using two of the colors twice. This will evenly distribute colors throughout the block.

3) **Stitch** rows together as shown, finger-pressing seams in opposite directions. Do not press.

4) **Stitch** one large triangle to the diagonal edge of pieced section, taking care not to stretch bias edges. Repeat on opposite edge. Press block, pressing seam allowances toward large triangles. Trim points that extend beyond block.

5) Repeat steps 2 to 4 for the remaining blocks; in step 2, randomly select two colors to be used twice. Arrange blocks, six across and four down, making sure that dark-colored triangles are next to light-colored solid triangles.

6) Stitch blocks into rows; stitch rows together, finger-pressing seam allowances in opposite directions. Press quilt top. Cut and attach border strips (pages 84 to 89); cut width of inner border strips is 1½" (3.8 cm) and cut width of outer border is 3½" (9 cm).

7) Cut backing about 4" (10 cm) larger than quilt top. Layer and baste quilt top, batting, and backing (pages 96 to 99). Quilt (pages 100 to 108).

8) Cut and apply binding (pages 112 and 113); cut width of binding is 2½" (6.5 cm). For wall hanging, attach fabric sleeve (page 165).

More Ocean Waves Designs

The Ocean Waves design illustrates how different color combinations can be used to create different effects. For a subtle look, combine a light-colored solid fabric in each triangle-square with a softly contrasting solid. For a more random effect, use eight light-colored and eight sharply contrasting dark-colored fabrics for the grid-pieced triangle-squares.

Design squares that are formed between the quilt blocks can be made from various fabrics, as shown in this quilt. The triangle-squares consist of a single light color and eight dark colors.

Subtle color variation is achieved in this quilt by using hand-dyed fabrics. A soft pink is used in each triangle-square, and eight shades of pinks, blues, and lavenders are used for the contrasting fabrics. The printed fabric unifies the design, and stipple quilting (page 106) adds texture throughout the quilt.

Vibrant pattern is created in this quilt by using scraps of eight light-colored and eight dark-colored fabrics for the triangle-squares.

Contemporary Crazy Quilts

This contemporary variation of crazy quilting looks intricate, but is actually quick and easy to piece. For a gradation of colors in the rows of the quilt blocks, hand-dyed fabrics work well for the background fabrics. Solid-colored and printed fabric strips that match the border fabrics are used for contrasting strips in the blocks.

The instructions that follow are for a wall hanging made from sixty-four 3" (7.5 cm) quilt blocks. The finished quilt with a double lapped border measures about 32" (81.5 cm) square.

✂ Cutting Directions

Cut four 2¼" × 18" (6 × 46 cm) strips from each hand-dyed fabric. Cut eight 1" (2.5 cm) crosswise strips from the fabric for the inner border; cut strips at the center foldline of the fabric to make 16 strips. Cut eight 1" (2.5 cm) strips from the fabric for the outer border. Cut one 3½" (9 cm) square template from heavy cardboard or plastic.

YOU WILL NEED

One hand-dyed fabric packet of eight fat quarters.

⅔ yd. (0.63 m) solid-colored fabric to be used for ¾" (2 cm) inner border and contrasting insert strip.

1 yd. (0.95 m) printed fabric to be used for 3" (7.5 cm) outer border and for contrasting insert strip.

1 yd. (0.95 m) fabric for backing.

Batting, about 36" (91.5 cm) square.

Heavy cardboard or plastic for template.

How to Make a Contemporary Crazy Quilt

1) Stitch two hand-dyed strips of the same color to each side of 1" (2.5 cm) strip from inner border fabric, right sides together. Repeat for remaining 15 strips. Press seam allowances toward center strip.

2) Cut four squares from each pieced strip, using template and rotary cutter; vary the angle of the strip on each square. Strips may be cut with three or four layers stacked together.

3) Set aside eight squares, one of each fabric color.

(Continued on next page)

4) Slash an angled cut through each remaining square, using straightedge; cut across insert strip and vary angle. Arrange corresponding portions in order, separating them in two stacks. Squares will be rejoined in step 7.

5) Stitch slashed edge of one portion from each square to edge of 1" (2.5 cm) strip from outer border fabric, right sides together; chainstitch portions together, extending the strip ½" (1.3 cm) beyond edges.

6) Press seam allowances toward strip. Trim ends of strip even with edges of squares, using straightedge or template as a guide.

7) Stitch corresponding portions of squares to the opposite edge of strips to make blocks. Press seam allowances toward center of strip, taking care not to stretch bias edges.

8) Arrange blocks into vertical rows of each color, turning contrasting strips in different directions; include blocks set aside in step 3, placing them in random positions within each row.

9) Stitch blocks of each color into rows; stitch rows together, finger-pressing seam allowances in opposite directions. Press quilt top.

10) Cut and attach border strips (pages 84 to 89); cut width of inner border strips is 1¼" (3.2 cm), and cut width of outer border strips is 3½" (9 cm).

11) Cut 36" (91.5 cm) square of backing fabric. Layer and baste quilt top, batting, and backing (pages 96 to 99).

12) Quilt around blocks and borders, using stitch-in-the-ditch method (pages 104 and 105). Cut and apply binding (pages 112 and 113); cut width of binding is 2" (5 cm). For wall hanging, attach fabric sleeve (page 165).

Tumbling Blocks

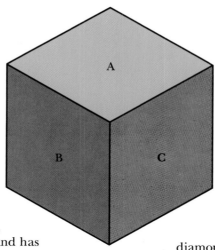

The Tumbling Blocks quilt design, also called Building Blocks and Baby's Blocks, allows for optical effects that are simple to achieve through the use of fabrics in light, medium, and dark colors. The blocks are placed with the light sides facing in the same direction for a three-dimensional look.

Tumbling Blocks are constructed using 60° diamonds. They can be cut quickly using a tool such as an Easy-Six™, designed for 60° diamonds. This tool eliminates any calculations and has markings for several sizes.

Three diamonds are stitched together to form a block unit. The blocks are joined at the sides in rows, and the rows are then stitched together. This quilt design does not lend itself to chainstitching; the blocks must be accurately pieced, one seam at a time, making this a more challenging project. For this reason, the Tumbling Blocks quilt design is usually used for smaller projects, such as wall hangings and crib quilts.

Tumbling Blocks quilts can be made with as few as three fabrics in light, medium, and dark colors or with a different fabric for every diamond in the quilt.

The instructions that follow are for a quilt made from diamonds with a finished width of 2" (5 cm). The finished quilt with a double lapped border measures about 25" × 40" (63.5 × 102 cm), a size suitable for a wall hanging or crib quilt.

✂ Cutting Directions

Cut 60° diamonds (below) from fabrics in light (**A**), medium (**B**), and dark (**C**) colors; use the markings on the tool for a finished width of 2" (5 cm). You will need 66 light-colored diamonds, 55 medium-colored diamonds, and 55 dark-colored diamonds.

YOU WILL NEED

³⁄₈ **yd. (0.35 m) fabric** each in light, medium, and dark colors; or scraps of fabrics in light, medium, and dark colors.

¹⁄₄ **yd. (0.25 m) fabric** for inner border.

¹⁄₂ **yd. (0.5 m) fabric** for outer border.

³⁄₈ **yd. (0.35 m) fabric** for binding.

1¹⁄₄ **yd. (1.15 m) fabric** for backing.

Batting, about 29" × 44" (73.5 × 112 cm).

How to Cut 60° Diamonds

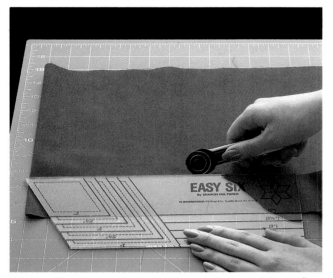

1) Cut the diamonds, using a tool designed for 60° diamonds. Cut fabric strips, using the marking for the desired finished size; strips will not measure finished size. To cut printed fabric, the tool and the fabric must be right sides up.

2) Trim selvage, using angled edge of tool. Rotate the tool, and place it at marking for desired finished size; cut along the angled edge of the ruler. Continue cutting additional diamonds from fabric strip.

How to Make a Tumbling Blocks Quilt

1) Mark wrong side of medium-colored diamonds where the 1/4" (6 mm) seams will intersect, placing a dot at one wide-angle corner of each diamond.

2) Align one medium-colored and one dark-colored diamond, right sides together, matching corners. Stitch from sharply pointed end exactly to the dot, with medium-colored diamond facing up; back-stitch to secure ends of stitching.

3) Align one side of a light-colored diamond to dark-colored diamond, right sides together, matching the edges and corners. Stitch from the pointed end exactly to the seam intersection, dark-colored diamond facing up; backstitch at ends.

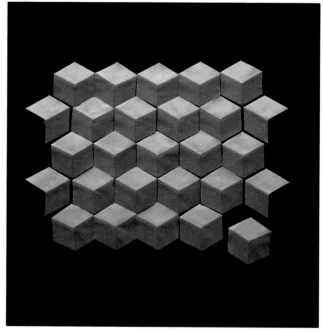

4) Align light-colored diamond to medium-colored diamond, right sides together; stitch seam as in step 3, with light-colored diamond facing up. Press lightly, pressing seams toward darker fabric. Trim points that extend beyond block.

5) Repeat steps 1 to 4 to make 50 blocks. Arrange blocks into rows, with light-colored diamond at top of each block. Piece the remaining diamonds into partial blocks, as shown, to complete the quilt top, making sure to use diamonds of correct colors.

6) Join the blocks side-by-side, beginning and ending all seams ¼" (6 mm) from edges; do not catch seam allowances in stitching. Backstitch at ends.

7) Join the rows in zigzag manner, stitching each individual seam and making sure not to catch the seam allowances in stitching; backstitch at ends.

8) Piece remaining light-colored diamonds at lower edge, as shown. Press quilt top, pressing seams toward darker fabric. Trim outer edges even, using straightedge and rotary cutter; allow ¼" (6 mm) seam allowances.

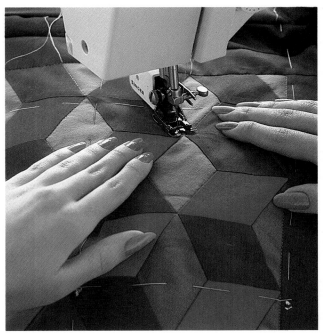

9) Cut and attach border strips (pages 84 to 89); cut width is 1¼" (3.2 cm) for inner border and 3½" (9 cm) for outer border. Cut backing 4" (10 cm) larger than the quilt top. Layer and baste the quilt top, batting, and backing (pages 96 to 99).

10) Quilt, using stitch-in-the-ditch method (pages 104 and 105); quilting may be done in horizontal rows, defining blocks. Cut and apply binding (pages 112 and 113); the cut width of the binding is 2½" (6.5 cm). For wall hanging, attach fabric sleeve (page 165).

More Tumbling Blocks Designs

The Tumbling Blocks design, with its dimensional quality, has many variations. Try turning some of the quilt blocks to create motion in the quilt design. Add subtle visual interest by using unexpected fabrics randomly.

Tumbling blocks can be built around six-pointed stars (pages 154 and 155). The stars and blocks are made individually, then arranged as desired before they are stitched together. The arrangement of the stars may be either symmetrical or random. You may want to experiment with different arrangements to create illusions, such as blocks suspended in space.

A design alternative is to stitch blocks into motifs, such as pyramids, and appliqué the motifs onto a quilt top, as on page 155. This is a faster way to incorporate Tumbling Blocks into larger quilts.

Three random stars, interspersed among the blocks, create an interesting visual effect. Scraps of solids, with an occasional print, are used to add variety.

Horizontal rows are emphasized in the quilt below by the use of color. Repetition adds unity to the quilt.

Pyramid of blocks is appliquéd onto a child's quilt. The blocks, arranged in different positions, create a tumbling illusion. The channel quilting adds dimension to the plain background fabric, and quilted block designs trim the border.

Stars and blocks in the quilt at right are arranged symmetrically in rows. Stipple quilting embellishes the stars and accentuates the three-dimensional quality of the blocks. The design is appliquéd onto a background fabric, forming an irregular border.

153

How to Make a Six-pointed Star

1) Cut diamonds the same size as the diamonds used for Tumbling Blocks (page 149), cutting six for each star. Mark diamonds where ¼" (6 mm) seams will intersect, placing a dot at each wide-angle corner.

2) Align two diamonds, right sides together, matching points. Stitch from one sharply pointed end exactly to dot; backstitch to secure ends of stitching.

3) Align a third diamond, matching raw edges and corners. Stitch from the dot to previous stitching; backstitch at ends.

4) Repeat steps 2 and 3, using the three remaining diamonds. Press seam allowances of each 3-diamond unit in same direction.

5) Place two 3-diamond units right sides together; pin, matching the seams at center. Stitch seam, beginning and ending ¼" (6 mm) from raw edge; backstitch at ends. Trim points that extend beyond edge.

6) Press from wrong side, working from center out, and pressing seam allowances in one direction.

How to Make a Tumbling Blocks Quilt with Six-pointed Stars

1) Make desired number of stars, opposite. Make desired number of Tumbling Blocks as on page 150, steps 1 to 4. Arrange blocks and stars as desired.

2) Add individual diamonds as necessary to fill in design around stars. Make and add partial blocks as on page 150, step 5.

3) Stitch units together, stitching each individual seam and backstitching at ends of seams. Whenever possible, stitch units together in rows, adding extra diamonds and stars as rows are joined.

4) Complete quilt as on page 151, steps 8 to 10; quilt around stars, then along blocks.

How to Apply a Tumbling Blocks Appliqué

1) Turn under ¼" (6 mm) at raw edges of the block motif; baste, then press in place.

2) Position design on quilt top as desired; pin or baste in place. Secure pressed edges as on page 173, step 5.

Sampler Quilt &
Related Projects

Pieced Heart Design

The quick piecing technique used to make the Pieced Heart quilt block actually yields two blocks. Two hearts are appliquéd to two background squares. Then the squares are cut and reassembled to make two 6" (15 cm) finished Pieced Heart blocks. Select two fabrics for the heart and two background fabrics that contrast.

A template made from cardboard or template material is used for shaping the heart appliqués. The hearts are applied to the background squares, using a technique called blindstitch appliqué (pages 172 and 173). For stitching that is almost invisible, use monofilament nylon thread in the needle and thread that matches the backing fabric in the bobbin.

Template for the Pieced Heart Design

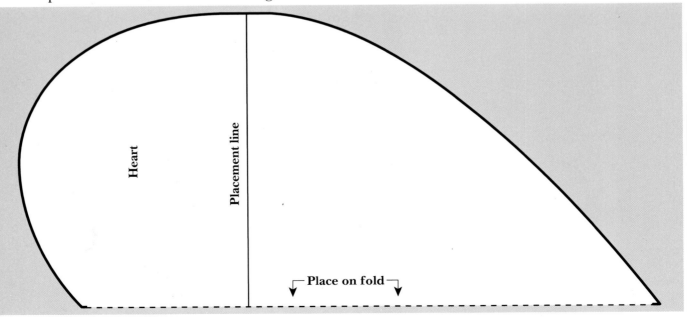

Heart

Placement line

← Place on fold →

How to Sew a Pieced Heart Block

1) Cut one 7¼" (18.7 cm) square each from two background fabrics.

2) Trace template (opposite) onto paper. Fold paper on dotted line; cut on outer solid line. Trace heart onto cardboard; transfer placement line to template. Cut out template.

3) Place template on heart fabric on the straight of grain. Adding ¼" (6 mm) seam allowance, cut around heart. Clip inside corner almost to template. Repeat to cut remaining heart from second fabric.

4) Spray starch in small bowl; dab starch on section of seam allowance. Place template on wrong side of heart. With tip of iron, press seam allowance over edge of template; using dry iron, press until spray starch dries. Continue pressing around heart. Turn heart over; press right side up.

5) Mark each side of heart appliqué at the placement line, on seam allowance, using marking pencil. Fold background square diagonally in both directions; press foldlines. Center heart diagonally on square, aligning placement marks with a foldline; pin in place. Repeat for remaining heart and background square.

6) Position tear-away stabilizer, cut larger than heart, on wrong side of background square. Appliqué the hearts to squares as on page 173, step 5. Remove stabilizer. Cut squares diagonally in both directions.

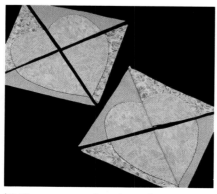

7) Rearrange triangles, alternating fabrics to make heart blocks. Using ¼" (6 mm) seams, stitch the upper heart triangles, right sides together; then stitch lower heart triangles together.

8) Stitch upper portion of heart to lower portion of heart, matching raw edges and finger-pressing seam allowances in opposite directions. Press block, pressing long seam allowances to one side.

Pieced Heart Quilts

This Pieced Heart quilt, used as a wall hanging or baby quilt, makes the perfect gift. Created from the Pieced Heart design (page 158), the finished quilt measures about 34" × 50" (86.5 × 127 cm). The quilt consists of fifteen heart blocks separated by sashing strips with connecting squares. To create a lasting memento of a special occasion, such as an anniversary, reunion, bridal or baby shower, make a friendship quilt by having family members or friends sign the quilt along the sashing strips.

The pieces of the heart blocks are assembled to make two styles of blocks. The Pieced Heart baby quilt opposite has blocks of various colors. Each block is made from two heart fabrics and two background fabrics. The blocks for the Pieced Heart wall hanging above are made using four fabrics for the hearts and two fabrics for the background.

For a friendship quilt, the signatures may be obtained before or after the quilt top is stitched together. Use a permanent-ink marking pen for the signatures, testing the pen by writing on a scrap of the sashing fabric and washing the fabric several times to see if the ink bleeds or fades. If you are collecting signatures on the sashing strips before the quilt top is assembled, prevent the fabric from slipping during signing by placing the strips on a piece of fine-grit sandpaper or

taping them to a piece of cardboard. You may also want to record on a sashing strip who the signers are, when the quilt was made, and if it was made for a special occasion.

✂ Cutting Directions

From each background fabric, cut two 7¼" (18.7 cm) strips; from the strips, cut eight 7¼" (18.7 cm) background squares of each fabric.

Make the heart template and cut sixteen hearts as on page 159, steps 2 and 3. For the baby quilt, cut two hearts from each of the eight heart fabrics; for the wall hanging, cut four hearts from each of the four heart fabrics.

Cut seven 2½" (6.5 cm) strips from sashing fabric; these will be cut to size for the sashing strips on page 162, step 4. Cut twenty-four 2½" (6.5 cm) squares from the heart fabrics; these will be used for the connecting squares in the sashing.

Cut four 4½" (11.5 cm) strips from the border fabric; these will be cut to size for the border strips on page 163, step 9. Cut four 4½" (11.5 cm) squares from one or more heart fabrics, to use for the corner squares of the border. Cut five 2½" (6.5 cm) strips from the binding fabric.

YOU WILL NEED

For a wall hanging:

$\frac{3}{8}$ yd. (0.35 m) each of four fabrics, for hearts, connecting squares of sashing, and corner squares of border.

$\frac{1}{2}$ yd. (0.5 m) each of two fabrics, for background.

$\frac{5}{8}$ yd. (0.6 m) fabric, for sashing.

$\frac{5}{8}$ yd. (0.6 m) fabric, for border.

$1\frac{1}{2}$ yd. (1.4 m) fabric, for backing.

$\frac{3}{8}$ yd. (0.35 m) fabric, for binding.

Batting, about 38" × 54" (96.5 × 137 cm).

$\frac{1}{3}$ yd. (0.32 m) muslin, for fabric sleeve, to hang quilt.

Lattice, for hanging quilt.

For a baby quilt:

$\frac{1}{4}$ yd. (0.25 m) each of eight fabrics, for hearts, connecting squares of sashing, and corner squares of border.

$\frac{1}{2}$ yd. (0.5 m) each of two fabrics, for background.

$\frac{5}{8}$ yd. (0.6 m) fabric, for sashing.

$\frac{5}{8}$ yd. (0.6 m) fabric, for border.

$1\frac{1}{2}$ yd. (1.4 m) fabric, for backing.

$\frac{3}{8}$ yd. (0.35 m) fabric, for binding.

Batting, about 38" × 54" (96.5 × 137 cm).

Pieced Heart design, used in an autographed wall hanging (opposite) or a pastel baby quilt (below), makes a perfect gift.

1) Prepare heart appliqués, stitch to background squares, and cut as on page 159, steps 3 to 6; stitch hearts from four fabrics to squares of one background fabric. Stitch hearts of remaining fabrics to squares of second background fabric.

2) Reassemble the triangles as on page 159, steps **7** and **8**, to make 16 blocks as shown.

3) Arrange blocks as desired into five rows of three blocks; there is one extra block that will not be used for the quilt.

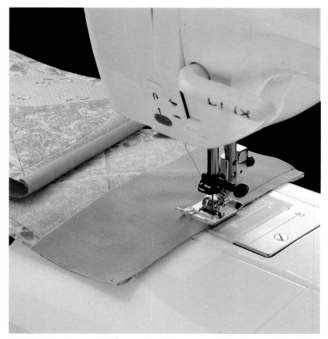

4) Measure sides of several quilt blocks to determine the shortest measurement; from the 2½" (6.5 cm) sashing strips, cut 38 strips to this length.

5) Stitch the sashing strips between blocks, right sides together, to form rows. Stitch strips to ends of rows. Press seam allowances toward sashing strips.

6) Stitch the remaining sashing strips alternately to the connecting squares to equal the length of the block-and-sashing row; there will be a connecting square at each end. Press seam allowances toward sashing strips.

7) Place one sashing unit along the lower edge of first block-and-sashing row, right sides together, matching seams. Pin along length, easing in any fullness; stitch. Repeat for remaining block-and-sashing rows.

8) Pin bottom of one row to top of a second row, as in step 7; stitch. Repeat to join remaining rows. Stitch sashing unit to upper edge of first row. Press seam allowances toward sashing units.

9) Measure the quilt top across the middle. From 4½" (11.5 cm) fabric strips, cut two border strips to this length. Measure the quilt top down the middle, from the top to the bottom; cut two border strips to this length.

(Continued on next page)

10) Pin upper border strip to upper edge of quilt top at center and ends, right sides together; pin along the length, easing any fullness. Stitch. Repeat at lower edge. Press seam allowances toward the border.

11) Stitch corner squares for border to ends of side border strips, right sides together. Finger-press seam allowances toward border strip.

12) Pin and stitch the pieced border strips to sides of quilt top, as in step 10, matching seamlines at corners. Press the seam allowances toward the border.

13) Cut backing fabric 4" (10 cm) wider and longer than quilt top. Layer and baste the quilt top, batting, and backing (pages 96 to 99). Quilt the wall hanging, using stitch-in-the-ditch method (pages 104 and 105). Stitch in seamlines of sashing and borders; then stitch an X through each Pieced Heart block.

14) Apply binding as on pages 112 and 113, using 2½" (6.5 cm) strips.

How to Sew a Pieced Heart Wall Hanging

1) Prepare heart appliqués, stitch to background squares, and cut as on page 159, steps 3 to 6; stitch two hearts from each fabric to two squares of each background fabric.

2) Reassemble the triangles as on page 159, steps 7 and 8, to make 16 blocks; in step 7, alternate triangles randomly, using four heart fabrics in each block. Complete quilt as on pages 162 to 164, steps 3 to 14. Attach fabric sleeve (below).

How to Hang a Quilt Using a Fabric Sleeve

1) Cut a piece of washed, unbleached muslin 6" (15 cm) wide by the width of the quilt. Turn under and stitch ½" (1.3 cm) double-fold hems at short ends.

2) Stitch long edges of strip, right sides together, in ½" (1.3 cm) seam; press seam allowances open. Turn sleeve right side out; press flat, centering seam.

3) Pin the sleeve to the back of the quilt, close to the top edge and 1" (2.5 cm) from the ends. Hand-stitch sleeve to quilt along upper and lower edges; stitch through backing and into batting.

4) Hang the quilt by inserting strip of sealed wooden lattice, cut ½" (1.3 cm) shorter than the width of the quilt, through sleeve. Secure lattice to wall, placing screws or nails at ends of lattice.

Ohio Star Design

The Ohio Star design is created from triangles and squares, and is made from three different fabrics. Select an obvious print for the center square. For the points of the star, use a fabric that is more dominant or darker than the fabric selected for the background. Star points with too little impact will fade into the background, making the center square appear to be the only design in the quilt block. You can make a 9" (23 cm) or 12" (30.5 cm) finished block with the instructions that follow. Both block sizes are used in the sampler quilts on pages 215 and 217. A larger Ohio Star block appears in the Birthday Banner on page 168.

How to Sew an Ohio Star Block

1a) For 9" (23 cm) finished block. Cut one 3½" (9 cm) square from the center square fabric and four 3½" (9 cm) squares from the background fabric. Cut two 4¼" (10.8 cm) squares each from star point fabric and background fabric.

1b) For 12" (30.5 cm) finished block. Cut one 4½" (11.5 cm) square from center square fabric and four 4½" (11.5 cm) squares from background fabric. Cut two 5¼" (13.2 cm) squares each from the star point fabric and background fabric.

2) Layer the four large squares, matching raw edges; cut through squares diagonally in both directions.

3) Align one star point triangle with one background triangle, right sides together. Stitch along one short side, taking care not to stretch bias edges; repeat for remaining units, using chainstitching (page 40).

4) Clip units apart; do not press. Place two units right sides together, alternating fabrics; finger-press seam allowances toward darker fabric. Stitch along long edge, taking care not to stretch bias edges. Repeat for remaining units, using chainstitching.

5) Clip the units apart; press the seams. Trim off the points.

6) Arrange the units into quilt block design as shown.

7) Assemble block, using chainstitching (page 40); finger-press seam allowances toward center square. Press block.

Ohio Star
Birthday Banners

This decorative wall banner features the Ohio Star design (page 166). Decorate a separate fabric square for each family member, and button it over the center of the banner to celebrate each person's birthday.

The lettering on the banner is stenciled onto the fabric before the quilt is assembled. For easy stencil designs, use the precut plastic alphabet stencils available in several sizes and styles at craft stores and office supply stores. Once stenciled, the personalized squares can be customized to each family member's interests with iron-on appliqués, embroidery, or even charms.

The finished banner measures about 31" (78.5 cm) square and hangs easily from a single nail.

✂ Cutting Directions

Cut five 8½" (21.8 cm) squares from background fabric. Cut two 9¼" (23.6 cm) squares each from star point fabric and background fabric; layer and cut the large squares as on page 167, step 2.

Cut three 4" (10 cm) strips from border fabric; trim each strip to 24½" (62.3 cm) in length for the side and lower border pieces. Cut two 1¼" (3.2 cm) strips from border fabric; trim each strip to 24½" (62.3 cm) in length for the narrow upper border pieces. The upper border piece with lettering is cut after the letters are stenciled. Cut four 4" (10 cm) squares from star point fabric for the corner squares of the border. For the binding, cut three 2" (5 cm) fabric strips.

For each personalized square, cut two 8½" (21.8 cm) squares from fabric and one 9½" (24.3 cm) square from thin batting or flannel.

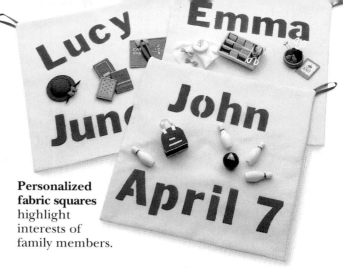

Personalized fabric squares highlight interests of family members.

YOU WILL NEED

⅝ yd. (0.6 m) fabric, for background.

⅓ yd. (0.32 m) fabric, for star points and corner squares of border.

⅔ yd. (0.63 m) fabric, for border and binding.

⅛ yd. (0.15 m) light-colored fabric, for upper border with lettering.

1 yd. (0.95 m) fabric, for backing.

Plastic or tear-away paper stencil.

Batting, about 35" (89 cm) square, for banner; thin batting or flannel, 9½" (24.3 cm) square, for each personalized square.

Fabric scraps, and 6" (15 cm) length of ribbon or cording, ⅛" (3 mm) wide, for each personalized square.

Two buttons.

Embellishments, for personalized squares.

Alphabet stencil, 1¼" to 1½" (3.2 to 3.8 cm) in height; fabric paints; disposable plates; stencil brush; medium-grit sandpaper.

Sawtooth picture hanger and 29" (73.5 cm) strip of sealed wooden lattice, for hanging banner.

How to Sew an Ohio Star Birthday Banner

1) Assemble Ohio Star block as on page 167, steps 3 to 7; in step 6, use square from background fabric for center square of block.

2) Determine spacing of border lettering on paper; finished length of border strip is 24" (61 cm). Mark letter spacing on a strip of tape; then position tape on fabric to use as a placement guide for letters.

(Continued on next page)

3) Place fabric, right side up, on sandpaper to keep fabric from shifting. Wrap tape around the bristles of stencil brush, ¼" (6 mm) from end. Position the first letter; apply tape to the surrounding cutout areas, if necessary to protect fabric.

4) Dip tip of stencil brush into fabric paint; blot onto folded paper towel until bristles are almost dry. Hold brush perpendicular to first letter, and apply paint, using an up-and-down motion. Repeat to stencil the remaining letters, repositioning stencil.

5) Heat-set fabric paint when it is dry, following the manufacturer's directions. Trim fabric to 2½" × 24½" (6.5 × 62.3 cm), taking care to center lettering.

6) Stitch the narrow border strips to upper and lower edges of stenciled border strip; press seam allowances toward the center.

7) Attach borders as on page 164, steps 10 to 12.

8) Mark quilting lines for template quilting on each corner square (page 102). Cut backing fabric 4" (10 cm) wider and longer than quilt top. Layer and baste the quilt top, batting, and backing (pages 96 to 99). Quilt, using the stitch-in-the-ditch method (pages 104 and 105) and the template method (pages 101 and 106).

9) Apply the binding as on pages 112 and 113.

10) Embellish right side of personalized fabric square as desired with flat embellishments. Pin 3" (7.5 cm) loop of ribbon or cording to each corner as shown.

11) Place embellished square and lining right sides together; place on batting, and pin layers together. Stitch ¼" (6 mm) from all edges, leaving a 3" (7.5 cm) opening on one side. Trim batting to ⅛" (3 mm); trim corners.

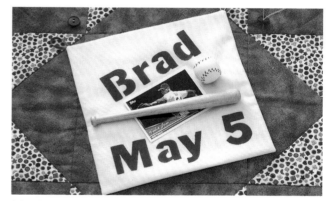

12) Turn square right side out; press lightly. Slipstitch the opening closed. Attach any three-dimensional embellishments as desired. Position the personalized square over center square of banner; mark position for buttons. Stitch buttons in place.

13) Cut fabric sleeve as on page 165, step 1; cut fabric strip in half to make two sleeves. Continue as on page 165, steps 1 to 3; in step 3, allow for 2" (5 cm) space at center of quilt in between fabric sleeves.

14) Insert a 29" (73.5 cm) strip of sealed wooden lattice through sleeves. Secure a sawtooth hanger to center of lattice. Hang banner from a nail.

Appliquéd Drunkard's Path Design

The smooth, curved design of the Drunkard's Path quilt block is easily accomplished, using a technique called blindstitch appliqué. A circle appliqué, made by shaping the fabric around a cardboard template, is stitched to a background square. The square is then cut into fourths to yield four pieced Drunkard's Path units.

The Drunkard's Path quilt design shown at left is called a sixteen-patch quilt block, because it is made from sixteen units. The units can be arranged in many ways to achieve a variety of designs. The instructions that follow are for a 12" (30.5 cm) sixteen-patch block. Other designs using the sixteen-patch Drunkard's Path block appear on pages 174 and 175.

Two fabrics are needed for the Drunkard's Path quilt block. Select one fabric for the background squares and a contrasting fabric for the circles. For invisible appliqué stitching, use monofilament nylon thread in the needle and thread that matches the backing fabric in the bobbin.

How to Sew a Sixteen-patch Drunkard's Path Quilt Block

1) Cut four 7" (18 cm) squares from the background fabric. Cut a 5" (12.5 cm) circle from heavy cardboard or template material, for template.

2) Place template on contrasting fabric. Adding scant ¼" (6 mm) seam allowance, cut around the template. Repeat to cut three more circles.

3) Spray starch in a small bowl; dab starch on fabric circle, on section of seam allowance. With tip of iron, press seam allowance over edge of template; press until spray starch dries. Continue pressing around circle. Remove template, and press circle right side up. Repeat for remaining circles.

4) Center the fabric circle on the background square, matching grainlines. Position tear-away stabilizer, cut larger than circle, on wrong side of background square; pin circle in place. Repeat for remaining circles.

5) Set machine for short blindstitch, with the stitch width about 1/16" (1.5 mm); use monofilament thread in the needle. Blindstitch around appliqué, catching edge with widest swing of the stitch. Repeat for the remaining circles. (Contrasting thread was used to show detail.)

6) Remove the tear-away stabilizer, taking care not to distort the stitches. Cut through center of square in both directions to make four Drunkard's Path units. Repeat for remaining squares.

7) Arrange the 16 units as shown, or choose from other block arrangements on page 175.

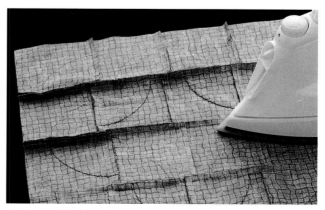

8) Assemble block, using chainstitching, as on page 40. Press block.

Drunkard's Path Placemats & Table Runners

Enhance a table with a set of quilted placemats and a table runner, using the Drunkard's Path design (page 172). For quick construction, the placemats and table runner are assembled using an easy stitch-and-turn method.

Each placemat is made from one sixteen-patch quilt block. Make all four placemats with the same sixteen-patch design, or add variety to the table setting by making each placemat with a different block design. Border strips, stitched to opposite sides of the block, are used to create a banded effect. The finished placemats measure about 12" × 18" (30.5 × 46 cm).

The table runner can be made in several lengths, depending on the number of Drunkard's Path blocks that are stitched together; a border strip is stitched to each end of the runner.

The table runner is most attractive when it is made from one block design, since the sixteen-patch block

arrangements form interesting designs when placed end to end. Experiment to see which design you like best by arranging the units in different ways before stitching the blocks. The instructions that follow are for a table runner of five sixteen-patch blocks. The finished table runner measures about 12" × 66" (30.5 × 168 cm).

✂ Cutting Directions (for four placemats)

Cut three 3½" (9 cm) strips from border fabric; cut the strips to make eight 3½" × 12½" (9 × 31.8 cm) rectangles for the border strips. Cut three 7" (18 cm) strips from background fabric; cut the strips to make sixteen 7" (18 cm) squares. Make the circle template, and cut sixteen 5" (12.5 cm) circles from fabric, as on page 172, steps 1 and 2.

Cut two 12½" (31.8 cm) strips from backing fabric; cut the strips to make eight 9½" × 12½" (24.3 × 31.8 cm) rectangles. Cut four 14½" × 20½" (36.8 × 52.3 cm) rectangles from batting.

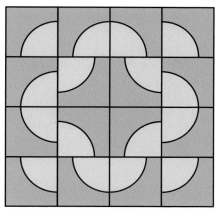

✂ Cutting Directions (for one table runner)

Cut two 3½" × 12½" (9 × 31.8 cm) rectangles from border fabric. Cut four 7" (18 cm) strips from background fabric; cut the strips to make twenty 7" (18 cm) squares. Make the circle template, and cut twenty 5" (12.5 cm) circles from fabric, as on page 172, steps 1 and 2.

Cut the backing fabric to make two 12½" × 34" (31.8 × 86.5 cm) strips. Cut one 14½" × 70" (36.8 × 178 cm) rectangle from batting.

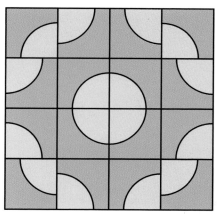

YOU WILL NEED

For four placemats:	**For one table runner:**
⅞ yd. (0.8 m) fabric, for circles and border strips.	⅝ yd. (0.6 m) fabric, for circles and border strips.
⅔ yd. (0.63 m) fabric, for background.	⅞ yd. (0.8 m) fabric, for background.
¾ yd. (0.7 m) fabric, for backing.	¾ yd. (0.7 m) fabric, for backing.
Low-loft quilt batting.	Low-loft quilt batting.
Tear-away stabilizer.	Tear-away stabilizer.

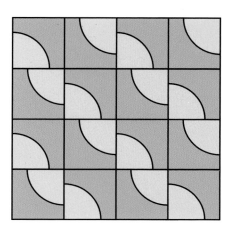

How to Sew a Drunkard's Path Placemat

1) Make the Drunkard's Path units as on page 173, steps 3 to 6.

2) Arrange 16 units, four across and four down, in the desired block arrangement, as shown on page 175.

3) Assemble the 16-patch block, using chainstitching (page 40).

4) Stitch a border strip to each end of block. Press the seam allowances toward borders.

5) Place two rectangles for backing with right sides together and raw edges even; stitch 1/4" (6 mm) seam on one long edge, leaving a 4" to 5" (10 to 12.5 cm) center opening for turning. Press seam open.

6) Place backing and placemat top right sides together. Center fabrics on batting, backing side up; pin or baste layers together.

7) Stitch around the placemat, ¼" (6 mm) from raw edges of fabric. Trim batting ⅛" (3 mm) from seam; trim corners diagonally.

8) Turn the placemat right side out; press lightly. Hand-stitch the opening closed.

9) Pin-baste layers together. Quilt placemat, using stitch-in-the-ditch method to define the borders and block (pages 104 and 105).

How to Sew a Drunkard's Path Table Runner

1) Follow steps 1 to 3, opposite, to make five 16-patch blocks in desired arrangement. Stitch blocks together end to end. Press seams open. Stitch a border strip to each end of the runner; press the seam allowances toward borders.

2) Follow step 5, opposite. Trim the backing to the length of the table runner top.

3) Complete the table runner as in steps 6 to 9, opposite. (Contrasting thread was used to show detail.)

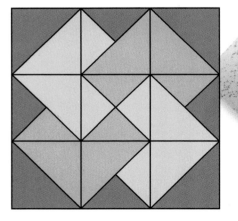

Card Trick Design

Three different pieced squares are used to make the Card Trick quilt block. The corner squares of the block are made from two triangles. The middle square on each side of the block is made from three triangles. And the center square of the block is made from four triangles. The instructions that follow are for Card Trick blocks in two sizes. The 9" (23 cm) finished

block is made using a background fabric and a different fabric for each of the four "cards." The 6" (15 cm) finished block is made using a background fabric and two card fabrics. Both block styles are used in the sampler quilt on page 215 and in the wall hanging on page 181.

How to Sew a 9" (23 cm) Card Trick Block Using Four Fabrics for the Cards

1) Cut one 4¼" (10.8 cm) square each from the background fabric and four card fabrics. Cut two 3⅞" (9.7 cm) squares from the background fabric and one from each of the four card fabrics.

2) Cut through the large squares diagonally in both directions. Cut through the small squares diagonally in one direction.

3) Arrange triangles from background and card fabrics as shown. There will be two triangles remaining from each of the four card fabrics.

4) Stitch background and card triangles of corner square, right sides together, on long sides, using chainstitching (page 40). Repeat for remaining corner squares.

5) Make middle square for side of block by stitching small background triangle to small card triangle on one short side. Then stitch pieced triangle to the remaining triangle for the middle square, stitching right sides together on long side. Repeat for remaining middle squares.

6) Stitch two small triangles for center square of block, right sides together, along one short side. Repeat for two remaining small triangles.

(Continued on next page)

How to Sew a 9" (23 cm) Card Trick Block Using Four Fabrics for the Cards (continued)

7) Complete center square of block by stitching pieced triangle sets right sides together, on long side, finger-pressing seam allowances in opposite directions. Trim off points.

8) Assemble block, using chainstitching (page 40). Press block.

How to Sew a 6" (15 cm) Card Trick Block Using Two Fabrics for the Cards

1) Cut one 3¼" (8.2 cm) square each from the background fabric and two card fabrics. Cut two 2⅞" (7.2 cm) squares each from background fabric and two card fabrics.

2) Cut through the large squares diagonally in both directions. Cut through the small squares diagonally in one direction.

3) Arrange the triangles from the background fabric and card fabrics as shown. Assemble as on pages 179 and 180, steps 4 to 7.

4) Assemble block, using chainstitching (page 40). Press block.

Card Trick Wall Hangings

This contemporary quilt, made using the Card Trick design (page 178), incorporates two quilt block sizes. Sashing pieces, cut from a coordinating fabric, are arranged for a random look and add interest to the block arrangement.

The wall hanging is made from six 9" (23 cm) Card Trick blocks and nine 6" (15 cm) Card Trick blocks. The finished quilt measures about 33" × 51" (84 ×

129.5 cm), making it suitable for a wall hanging, baby quilt, or small lap quilt.

To add interest to the quilt, choose a narrow-striped fabric for the sashing pieces. This gives vertical and horizontal movement to the design. To unify the quilt design, you may want to use one of the card fabrics for the border of the quilt.

✂ Cutting Directions

For the 9" (23 cm) finished blocks, cut the following strips across the width of the fabric: one 4¼" (10.8 cm) strip each from the background fabric and the four card fabrics; two 3⅞" (9.7 cm) strips from the background fabric; and one 3⅞" (9.7 cm) strip each from the four card fabrics. Cut the strips to make six 4¼" (10.8 cm) squares from the background fabric, three 4¼" (10.8 cm) squares from each of the card fabrics, twelve 3⅞" (9.7 cm) squares from the background fabric, and six 3⅞" (9.7 cm) squares from each of the card fabrics. Cut the squares diagonally as on page 179, step 2, cutting the large squares in both directions and cutting the small squares in one direction.

For the 6" (15 cm) finished blocks, cut the following strips: one 3¼" (8.2 cm) strip each from the background fabric and the four card fabrics; two 2⅞" (7.2 cm) strips from the background fabric; one 2⅞" (7.2 cm) strip each from the four card fabrics. Determine the desired arrangement of card fabrics for each of the nine 6" (15 cm) blocks. Cut strips into the necessary triangles for each block as on page 180, steps 1 and 2.

For the sashing, cut four 3½" (9 cm) strips. Cut the strips to make nine 3½" × 6½" (9 × 16.3 cm) rectangles and nine 3½" × 9½" (9 × 24.3 cm) rectangles.

For the border, cut five 3½" (9 cm) strips. The strips will be cut to size for the border strips in step 9, right. For the binding, cut four 2½" (6.5 cm) fabric strips.

YOU WILL NEED

½ yd. (0.5 m) each of four fabrics, for cards of Card Trick blocks.

⅝ yd. (0.6 m) fabric, for background of Card Trick blocks.

½ yd. (0.5 m) fabric, for sashing.

½ yd. (0.5 m) fabric, for border.

1½ yd. (1.4 m) fabric, for backing.

½ yd. (0.5 m) fabric, for binding.

Batting, about 39" × 55" (99 × 139.5 cm).

How to Sew a Card Trick Wall Hanging

1) Make six 9" (23 cm) finished Card Trick blocks as on pages 179 and 180, steps 3 to 7.

2) Make three 6" (15 cm) finished Card Trick blocks as on page 180, steps 3 and 4.

5) Stitch one long sashing strip to lower edge of one small block-and-sashing unit, right sides together; press seam allowances toward sashing strip. Repeat for six additional blocks. This gives you seven square units and two rectangular units.

8) Stitch the units together to make three rows; press seam allowances toward sashing strips. Stitch rows together; press seam allowances to one side. Press quilt top.

9) Cut and apply the border as for inner border on page 199, steps 3 to 5; consider short ends of this quilt to be upper and lower edges for this step.

3) Repeat step 2 twice, using a different combination of card fabrics for each set of three blocks. This gives you three sets of three blocks.

4) Stitch one short sashing strip to one side of one small block, right sides together; press seam allowances toward sashing strip. Repeat for remaining small blocks.

6) Stitch one long sashing strip to one side of one large block, right sides together; press seam allowances toward sashing strip. Repeat for a second block and long sashing strip.

7) Arrange blocks into three rows as shown. Reposition or turn blocks as necessary for pleasing overall design.

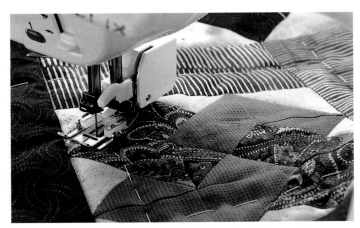

10) Cut backing fabric 4" (10 cm) wider and longer than quilt top. Layer and baste quilt top, batting, and backing (pages 96 to 99). Quilt, using stitch-in-the-ditch method (pages 104 and 105).

11) Apply binding as on pages 112 and 113.

Spools Design

The four-patch Spools quilt block consists of four spool blocks. Each spool block is made from four trapezoids and one center square. Two trapezoids become the upper and lower portions of the spool, and the remaining two trapezoids become the background in the block. The center square is cut from striped fabric to represent the thread on the spool.

For best results, cut the trapezoids for the spools and the squares for the thread from fabrics that are similar in color value. Cut the background trapezoids from a fabric that strongly contrasts with the fabrics used for the spools and thread. The trapezoids can be cut using a quilter's tool, such as the Companion Angle™, or they can be cut using the template, below.

The instructions that follow are for a 9" (23 cm) finished four-patch block. The block is used in the sampler quilts (pages 215 and 217), the Spools wall hanging (page 187), and the tote bag (page 240).

Template for the Spools Design

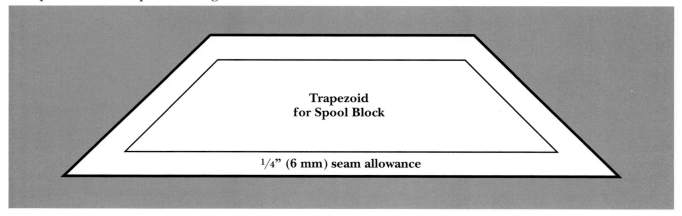

Trapezoid
for Spool Block

¼" (6 mm) seam allowance

How to Sew a Four-patch Spools Block

1) Cut four 3" (7.5 cm) squares from striped fabric for thread. Cut one 1½" (3.8 cm) strip each from spool fabric and background fabric; layer strips, matching raw edges.

2a) Quilter's tool. Align 5" (12.5 cm) dotted line on Companion Angle with one long side of layered strips; cut along angled edges of tool. To cut second set of trapezoids, rotate tool and align it with diagonal cut edge of fabric; cut. Repeat to cut eight trapezoids from each color.

2b) Template. Make the template (opposite) from cardboard or from template material. Align template with raw edges of fabric strips; mark along angled sides, using chalk or marking pencil. To mark second set of trapezoids, rotate and realign the tool. Repeat to mark eight sets of trapezoids. Cut on marked lines.

3) Mark wrong side of each thread square where the ¼" (6 mm) seams will intersect, placing a dot at each corner. Pin-mark center of each side of thread square. Pin-mark center of shortest long edge of spool and background trapezoids.

4) Align spool trapezoid to thread square, matching pin marks, with edge of trapezoid parallel to stripes of the thread square. Stitch exactly between the dots, backstitching at beginning and end of stitching. Repeat on opposite side of square.

(Continued on next page)

How to Sew a Four-patch Spools Block (continued)

5) Finger-press seam allowances toward the trapezoids. Repeat step 4 to stitch the background trapezoids to the thread square.

6) Align angled ends of two adjacent trapezoids, right sides together. Stitch from the pointed end exactly to the seam intersection; backstitch. Repeat at remaining corners. Press seams of background trapezoids toward spool trapezoids and thread square; trim points.

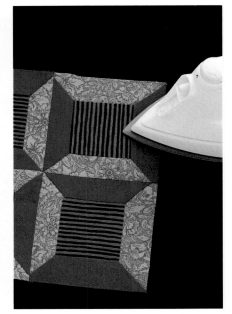

7) Continue as on pages 185 and 186, steps 3 to 6, to make four spool blocks. Stitch two blocks together, in a vertical-horizontal arrangement as shown. Finger-press seam allowances to one side.

8) Stitch remaining two squares together in a horizontal-vertical arrangement as shown. Finger-press seam allowances in opposite direction from first row.

9) Stitch the two rows together, matching seamlines. Finger-press seam allowances to one side. Press the quilt block.

Spools Wall Hangings

A decorative wall hanging, made from the Spools design (page 184), can have a country or homespun look. It may have special appeal to a person who sews. For extra detail, the border incorporates a spool block at each corner. Striped fabric is used to represent the thread on the spools. To achieve several color variations with the same striped fabric, the fabric can be overdyed, using fabric dye according to the manufacturer's instructions.

The border of the wall hanging can be embellished, if desired, with buttons of various sizes, arranged randomly. The finished wall hanging measures about 42" (107 cm) square.

✂ Cutting Directions

In the directions that follow, cut the strips across the width of the fabric. Cut ten 1½" (3.8 cm) strips from the spool fabric; cut the strips to make 80 spool trapezoids as on page 185; step 2a or 2b. Cut nine 1½" (3.8 cm) strips from the background fabric; cut the strips to make 72 background trapezoids. Cut one 1½" (3.8 cm) strip from the inner border fabric; cut the strip to make eight background trapezoids for the corner blocks of the border.

Cut three 3" (7.5 cm) strips from thread fabric; cut the strips to make 40 thread squares, each 3" × 3" (7.5 × 7.5 cm).

Cut four 2" (5 cm) strips from the inner border fabric; these will be cut to length in step 5, opposite. Cut four 5" (12.5 cm) strips from the outer border fabric;

these will be cut to length for the borders in step 6. Cut four 2½" (6.5 cm) strips from the binding fabric.

YOU WILL NEED

Striped fabric, for thread, one or more colors to total about ⅓ yd. (0.32 m).

½ yd. (0.5 m) fabric, for spools.

½ yd. (0.5 m) fabric, for background.

¼ yd. (0.25 m) fabric, for inner border and for background trapezoids of corner spool blocks.

1 yd. (0.95 m) fabric, for outer border and binding.

1½ yd. (1.4 m) fabric, for backing.

Batting, about 46" (117 cm) square.

Buttons, about 50 in various sizes and colors, optional.

How to Sew a Spools Wall Hanging

1) Complete nine four-patch Spools blocks as on pages 185 and 186.

2) Stitch four spool blocks for border, using trapezoids cut from the inner border fabric for the background trapezoids; set aside.

3) Arrange four-patch blocks as desired into three rows of three blocks.

4) Stitch blocks into rows; then stitch rows together, finger-pressing seam allowances in opposite directions. Press quilt top.

5) Continue as on page 199, steps 3 to 5; in step 5, omit reference to piecing inner border.

6) Measure through middle of quilt in both directions to determine the shortest measurement. Trim four 5" (12.5 cm) outer border fabric strips to this length.

7) Attach the border as on page 164, steps 10 to 12, positioning corner spools upright.

8) Cut backing fabric 4" (10 cm) wider and longer than quilt top. Layer and baste the quilt top, batting, and backing (pages 96 to 99).

9) Quilt the wall hanging, using the stitch-in-the-ditch method (pages 104 and 105). Stitch in the seamlines of inner and outer borders; then stitch between blocks and around the spools to define design. (Contrasting thread was used to show detail.)

10) Apply binding as on pages 112 and 113. Stitch buttons to border, placing buttons randomly. Attach fabric sleeve (page 165).

The Shadowed Square quilt block, illustrated in the graphic above right, is made from two triangles. One triangle is cut from strip-pieced fabrics and the other from a coordinating fabric. Four 6" (15 cm) blocks can be assembled to make a 12" (30.5 cm) diamond design as shown above. This design is used in the sampler quilts on pages 215 and 217 and in the pillow on page 192. The Shadowed Square block and variations of it are also used in the lap quilt on page 195.

Strip piecing, stitching fabric strips together side by side, makes interesting striped fabric from which to cut triangles. A quilter's tool, such as the Companion Angle™, can be used to cut the triangles quickly. Or, cut them using a template made from cardboard or template material. To save fabric, the tool or the template can be rotated to cut every other triangle. This produces two variations of strip-pieced triangles. For the diamond design, use four matching triangles.

How to Sew Shadowed Square Quilt Blocks

1) Cut one 1½" (3.8 cm) strip across the width of five different fabrics. Stitch strips right sides together, lengthwise, in desired sequence, using ¼" (6 mm) seam allowances.

2) Place pieced strip across, rather than lengthwise, on ironing surface, to prevent distorting grainline during pressing. Press all the seam allowances in one direction, or, for a seam joining a light and a dark fabric, press seam allowances toward the dark fabric. Turn strip over, and press from the right side.

3a) Quilter's tool. Align 9" (23 cm) dotted line on Companion Angle with one long edge of the pieced strip; cut along angled edges of tool. Rotate tool and align with opposite raw edge to cut second triangle. Repeat to cut additional triangles.

3b) Template. Cut a 6⅞" (17.5 cm) square from cardboard or template material, and cut it in half diagonally to make triangle template. Align long edge of template with raw edge of pieced strip; mark along angled sides, using marking pencil. Rotate and realign template to mark second triangle. Repeat to mark additional triangles; cut triangles.

4) Cut 6⅞" (17.5 cm) squares from coordinating fabric. Layer squares, and cut in half diagonally to make triangles.

5) Align coordinating fabric triangle and strip-pieced triangle, right sides together; stitch on long edge, taking care not to stretch bias edges. Finger-press seam allowance toward darker fabric.

How to Sew a Diamond Design from Shadowed Square Quilt Blocks

1) Follow steps 1 to 5, opposite; make four Shadowed Square blocks, using identical strip-pieced triangles. Arrange blocks to form a center diamond as shown.

2) Stitch blocks to form two rows; then stitch the rows together, finger-pressing seam allowances in opposite directions. Press block, pressing long seam allowances to one side.

Shadowed Square Pillows

For a quick quilting project, make a pillow using the Shadowed Square design on page 190. This pillow features a diamond design framed by a 3" (7.5 cm) coordinating border.

The pillow cover is designed to fit an 18" (46 cm) pillow form. For easy construction, the pillow cover back has an overlap closure, secured with hook and loop tape.

✂ Cutting Directions

For the pillow cover front, cut two 3½" × 12½" (9 × 31.8 cm) border strips and two 3½" × 18½" (9 × 47.3 cm) border strips. Also cut two 18½" × 13" (47.3 × 33 cm) rectangles, for the pillow cover back.

YOU WILL NEED

¼ yd. (0.25 m) each of four fabrics, for stripes of diamond.

⅝ yd. (0.6 m) fabric, for one stripe of diamond, border strips, and pillow back.

¼ yd. (0.25 m) fabric, for background.

⅝ yd. (0.6 m) muslin, for pillow lining.

Batting, about 20" (51 cm) square.

One 18" (46 cm) square pillow form.

2" (5 cm) strip of hook and loop tape, ¾" (2 cm) wide.

How to Sew a Shadowed Square Pillow

1) Cut and assemble four Shadowed Square blocks into diamond design as on pages 190 and 191. Stitch one short border strip to one side of block, right sides together and raw edges even. Press seam allowances toward border. Repeat on opposite side.

2) Stitch remaining border strips to the remaining sides of block. Press seam allowances toward the border. Press pieced pillow top.

3) Place batting over muslin. Center pieced pillow top, right side up, over batting; baste layers together (pages 96 to 99). Quilt the block, using the stitch-in-the-ditch method (pages 104 and 105).

4) Press under 1" (2.5 cm) twice on one long edge of the rectangle for pillow back; stitch to make double-fold hem. Repeat for the remaining pillow back piece.

5) Position pillow back piece over the pillow front, right sides together, matching raw edges; hemmed edges of the back pieces overlap about 3" (7.5 cm) at center. Pin in place.

6) Stitch around pillow cover, ¼" (6 mm) from raw edges. Trim the batting ⅛" (3 mm) from seam. Trim muslin even with edges of pillow cover. Trim corners diagonally. Turn pillow right side out; press lightly.

7) Pin hook side of hook and loop tape to overlap, centering tape on hem; stitch around tape. Pin loop side of hook and loop tape to the underlap, directly under hook side of tape; stitch.

8) Insert the pillow form into pillow cover. Secure the hook and loop tape.

Shadowed Square Lap Quilts

Although this lap quilt appears intricate, it is actually simple to sew. It is made using the Shadowed Square design with a diagonal strip-pieced triangle (page 190) and several variations; half of each block is a plain fabric triangle. Easy strip-piecing techniques are used to assemble the pieced triangle designs.

Choose a printed fabric for the plain fabric triangles in each of the blocks. Then choose eight or more coordinating fabrics to use for the pieced triangles. Printed fabrics and fabrics with color gradations will make the finished quilt appear more intricate. The finished quilt with a double border measures about 44" × 56" (112 × 142 cm).

✂ Cutting Directions

In the directions that follow, cut the strips across the width of the fabric. Cut four 6⅞" (17.5 cm) strips from printed fabric; cut the strips to make twenty-four 6⅞" (17.5 cm) squares. Cut the squares diagonally as on page 191, step 4, to make 48 triangles. The fabric strips for the pieced triangles are cut on pages 196 to 198.

Cut five 1½" (3.8 cm) strips from inner border fabric. Cut five 3½" (9 cm) strips from outer border fabric. The strips will be cut to length for the inner and outer borders on page 199. Cut five 2½" (6.5 cm) strips from binding fabric.

YOU WILL NEED

1 yd. (0.95 m) printed fabric, for plain triangles.
⅓ yd. (0.32 m) each of eight or more coordinating fabrics, for pieced triangles.
⅓ yd. (0.32 m) fabric, for inner border.
⅔ yd. (0.63 m) fabric, for outer border.
½ yd. (0.5 m) fabric, for binding.
Batting, about 48" × 60" (122 × 152.5 cm) rectangle.
2⅔ yd. (2.48 m) fabric, for backing.

The Shadowed Square lap quilt (opposite) is made using the basic Shadowed Square block and several variations.

Block with diagonal strip-pieced triangle.

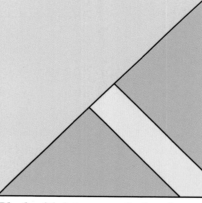

Block with interrupted triangle (version one).

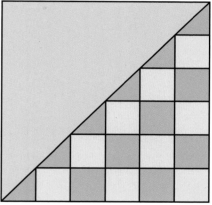

Block with 1" (2.5 cm) checkerboard triangle.

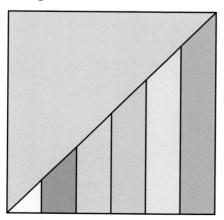

Block with vertical strip-pieced triangle.

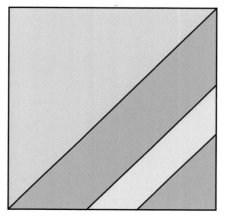

Block with interrupted triangle (version two).

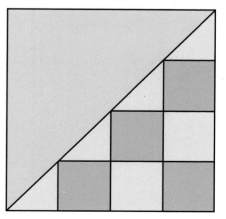

Block with 1½" (3.8 cm) checkerboard triangle.

How to Sew the Blocks for the Shadowed Square Lap Quilt

Diagonal strip-pieced triangles. Cut and assemble eight strip-pieced triangles, as on pages 190 and 191, steps 1 to 3. Repeat to make eight additional triangles, using different fabrics or a different arrangement of the fabrics for the pieced strip.

Vertical strip-pieced triangles. 1) Cut one 1½" (3.8 cm) strip each from six fabrics. Stitch the strips together lengthwise in scant ¼" (6 mm) seams in the desired sequence. Press seam allowances in one direction.

2) Cut eight triangles from pieced strip as on page 191, step 3a or 3b; align short edge of template with the raw edge of pieced strip. Point of triangle extends slightly beyond one edge of pieced strip.

Interrupted triangles. 1) Cut one 5" (12.5 cm) strip from fabric; cut one 1½" (3.8) strip from a different fabric. Cut strips in half; discard one narrow strip.

2) Stitch a 5" (12.5 cm) strip to each side of narrow strip, in ¼" (6 mm) seams. Press seam allowances toward center strip.

3) Repeat steps 1 and 2 to make a second pieced strip, using different fabrics.

4) Mark four triangles on each pieced strip, using template or tool; vary the position of the template so the narrow fabric strip runs both horizontally and vertically across the triangles. Cut triangles.

How to Sew the Blocks for the Shadowed Square Lap Quilt

1" (2.5 cm) checkerboard triangles. 1) Cut two 1½" (3.8 cm) strips each from two contrasting fabrics; cut the strips in half. Stitch six strips together lengthwise, in scant ¼" (6 mm) seams, alternating fabrics. Press strip, pressing seam allowances in one direction.

2) Repeat step 1, using different fabrics, to make a second pieced strip. Trim the short end of each strip at a 90° angle. Cut 1½" (3.8 cm) strips across each pieced fabric strip.

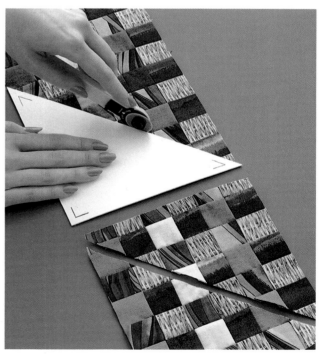

3) Stitch pieced strips together in scant ¼" (6 mm) seams, alternating them to form a checkerboard. Press seam allowances in one direction.

4) Mark eight triangles on strip, using a template or a tool, and aligning short edge of template with raw edge of pieced strip. Point of triangle extends slightly beyond pieced strip. Cut triangles.

(Continued on next page)

How to Sew the Blocks for the Shadowed Square Lap Quilt (continued)

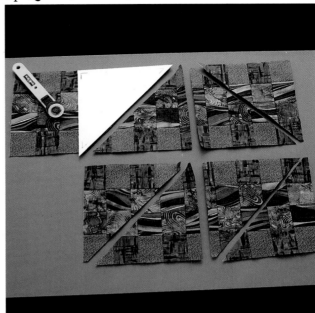

1½" (3.8 cm) checkerboard triangles. 1) Cut one 2" (5 cm) strip each from four fabrics. Stitch the strips together lengthwise in scant ¼" (6 mm) seams. Press seam allowances in one direction.

2) Cut 2" (5 cm) strips across pieced strip as on page 197, step 2. Reassemble strips, alternating fabrics to form a checkerboard. Cut eight triangles from strip as shown.

How to Assemble the Shadowed Square Lap Quilt

1) Place pieced triangle and plain fabric triangle right sides together; stitch on long edge, taking care not to stretch bias edges. Press the seam allowances toward plain triangle; trim points. Repeat to make 48 blocks.

2) Arrange blocks six across and eight down, rotating plain triangles to create a radiating diamond pattern. Stitch the blocks into rows; then stitch rows together, finger-pressing seam allowances in opposite directions. Press quilt top.

3) Measure the quilt top across the middle. Cut two inner border strips equal to this measurement, for upper and lower inner border.

4) Pin inner border strip to upper edge of quilt top at center and ends, right sides together; pin along length, easing in any fullness. Stitch; press the seam allowances toward inner border. Press from right side. Repeat at lower edge.

5) Piece remaining inner border strips; trim seam allowances. Measure quilt top down the middle, including inner border strips. Cut two inner border strips for sides equal to this length. Pin and stitch the strips to sides of quilt top as in step 4.

6) Repeat steps 3 to 5 to apply the outer border. Cut backing fabric 4" (10 cm) wider and longer than quilt top, piecing as necessary.

7) Layer and baste the quilt as on pages 96 to 99. Quilt, using stitch-in-the-ditch method (pages 104 and 105). Apply the binding as on pages 112 and 113.

Nine-patch &
Double Nine-patch Designs

A Nine-patch quilt block, made from nine squares, is one of the most basic quilt blocks. The Double Nine-patch block alternates squares and checkerboard pieced squares. Each of the checkerboard squares is made from nine smaller squares.

Both styles of blocks are used in the sampler quilts on pages 215 and 217. One of these blocks is also used to make the sleeping bag on page 203, and the other is used for the coordinating tote bag on page 241.

The checkerboard squares used in the Double Nine-patch block are made using a strip-piecing method that lets you create intricate designs quickly without individually seaming small pieces of fabric.

The instructions that follow are for a 6" (15 cm) Nine-patch block and a 9" (23 cm) Double Nine-patch block. At least two fabrics are needed to make each quilt block.

How to Sew a Nine-patch Quilt Block

1) Cut five 2½" (6.5 cm) squares from Fabric A, and cut four 2½" (6.5 cm) squares from Fabric B.

2) Arrange the squares, alternating the fabrics, to form a nine-square checkerboard.

3) Assemble the quilt block, using chainstitching (page 40). Press the block.

How to Sew a Double Nine-patch Quilt Block

1) Cut four 3½" (9 cm) squares from Fabric A. Cut two 1½" (3.8 cm) strips across the width of both Fabric A and Fabric B; cut strips in half to make four strips of each.

2) Stitch one B-A-B unit and one A-B-A unit, right sides together. Discard remaining two strips. Press all of the seams toward the darker fabric.

3) Trim short end of each pieced strip at a 90° angle. Cut ten 1½" (3.8 cm) strips across B-A-B unit and five 1½" (3.8 cm) strips across A-B-A unit.

4) Stitch one B-A-B unit to one A-B-A unit on the long edges, right sides together. Then stitch B-A-B unit to the other long edge of A-B-A unit, right sides together, to form checkerboard. Repeat to make four more checkerboard units. Press the seam allowances toward the sides with the two darker squares.

5) Alternate plain squares with checkerboard squares to form the Double Nine-patch block. Assemble block, using chainstitching (page 40).

Nine-patch Sleeping Bags

Children will love snuggling down into their own patchwork sleeping bag, made with the Nine-patch design (page 200). A generous side opening makes it easy to get in and out of the sleeping bag.

Novelty printed fabrics, combined with a solid coordinating fabric, work well for the Nine-patch design in this project. The Nine-patch quilt blocks are separated by sashing with connecting squares. The connecting squares of the sashing can be cut from the primary fabric in the block to create a dominant diagonal effect.

Several timesaving techniques are used to construct the sleeping bag. The Nine-patch blocks on the front of the sleeping bag are stitched together quickly, using strip-piecing. Simple stitch-in-the-ditch quilting is used on the front of the sleeping bag; however, to save time and give a more intricate look to the piecing, the stitching is continued from block to block by stitching through the sashing. The back of the sleeping bag is constructed from one fabric piece and features channel quilting.

The instructions that follow are for a finished sleeping bag that measures about 34" × 58" (86.5 × 147 cm). A shorter bag, about 50" (127 cm) in length, can be made by eliminating one row of blocks and sashing. For convenience, the sleeping bag features ties at the lower edges so the bag may be rolled up and tied in a neat bundle.

✂ Cutting Directions

Cut the following strips across the width of the fabric: eleven 2½" (6.5 cm) strips from the primary fabric in the block and eight 2½" (6.5 cm) strips from the secondary fabric in the block. These pieces will be strip-pieced and cut to make the Nine-patch blocks.

Cut twelve 2½" (6.5 cm) strips from the sashing fabric; these will be cut to size for the sashing strips as on page 204, step 4. Cut two 2½" (6.5 cm) strips from the fabric for the connecting squares of the sashing; cut the strips to make forty 2½" (6.5 cm) squares.

Trim the width of the fabric for the back to 38" (96.5 cm). Cut two 38" × 62" (96.5 × 157.5 cm) pieces from the inner lining fabric. The sleeping bag lining is cut after the outer bag is constructed.

YOU WILL NEED

⅞ yd. (0.8 m) printed fabric, for primary fabric in block.

⅔ yd. (0.63 m) fabric, for secondary fabric in block.

1 yd. (0.95 m) fabric, for sashing.

¼ yd. (0.25 m) fabric, for connecting squares of sashing.

1¾ yd. (1.6 m) fabric, for back of sleeping bag.

3⅓ yd. (3.07 m) muslin, for inner lining.

3⅓ yd. (3.07 m) fabric, for lining.

Batting, two pieces about 38" × 62" (96.5 × 157.5 cm).

2⅝ yd. (2.4 m) grosgrain ribbon, ⅝" (1.5 cm) wide, for ties.

How to Sew a Nine-patch Sleeping Bag

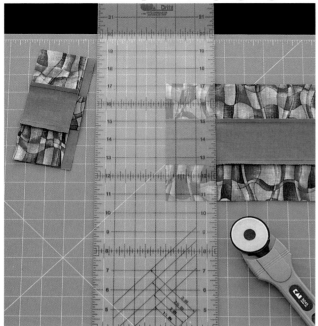

1) **Stitch** four B-A-B units and two A-B-A units, as for Double Nine-patch quilt block on page 201, step 2. Trim short end of each pieced unit at 90° angle. Cut 2½" (6.5 cm) strips across each pieced unit.

2) **Stitch** one B-A-B unit to one A-B-A unit on long edges, right sides together. Then stitch B-A-B unit to other long edge of A-B-A unit, right sides together, to form checkerboard. Press seam allowances toward the sides with the two darker squares.

3) **Repeat** step 2 to make 28 quilt blocks. Arrange the blocks, four across and seven down.

4) **Measure** sides of several quilt blocks to determine shortest measurement; using 2½" (6.5 cm) sashing fabric strips, cut 67 sashing strips to this length.

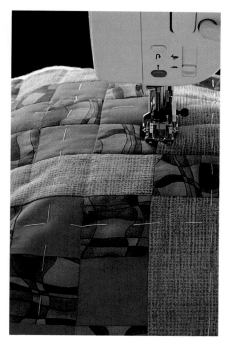

5) Attach sashing with connecting squares as on pages 162 and 163, steps 5 to 8.

6) Layer and baste the sleeping bag front, batting, and inner lining (pages 96 to 99).

7) Quilt, using stitch-in-the-ditch method (pages 104 and 105), stitching continuous rows through sashing.

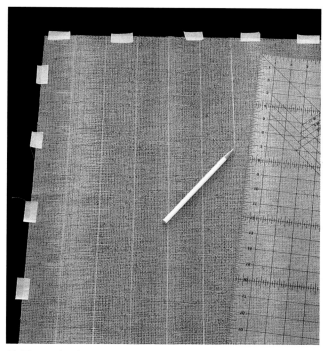

8) Trim batting and inner lining even with edge of the pieced top. Measure the front of the sleeping bag across and down the middle; record dimensions for use in step 14.

9) Tape the backing fabric to a hard, flat work surface, keeping fabric smooth and taut. Using a straightedge and quilting pencil, mark 2" (5 cm) parallel lines down length of fabric for backing. Remove tape.

(Continued on next page)

10) Layer and baste sleeping bag back, batting, and inner lining. Channel-quilt (pages 104 and 105) on the marked lines; reverse the direction of stitching every other line to avoid distorting fabric.

11) Trim back of sleeping bag to same size as front. Cut two 46" (117 cm) lengths of ribbon; fold each length in half, and pin to lower edge of sleeping bag back, 4½" (11.5 cm) and 12½" (31.8 cm) from one side. Stitch ribbon to bag, scant ¼" (6 mm) from raw edge.

12) Pin the sleeping bag front to sleeping bag back, with right sides together and raw edges even. Pin-mark 18" (46 cm) from upper edge for opening on one side of sleeping bag.

13) Stitch around sides and bottom, backstitching at pin mark for opening. Clip the seam allowances at backstitching. Turn right side out.

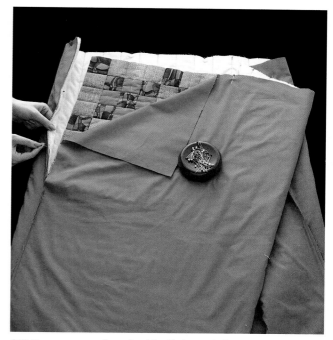

14) Cut two lining pieces to dimensions of sleeping bag front; pin right sides together. Pin-mark side opening, and stitch as for outer section, leaving a 12" (30.5 cm) center opening on lower edge for turning; do not clip seam allowances at backstitching. Do not turn right side out.

15) Insert outer bag inside lining, right sides together; pin along side opening and upper edge, with the raw edges even. Stitch, beginning and ending at bottom of side opening.

16) Turn the sleeping bag right side out through opening in bottom of lining. Edgestitch opening closed.

17) Insert lining inside the sleeping bag. Tack lining to bottom of outer bag at lower seam.

18) Press lightly on upper edge and side opening edges. Topstitch ¼" (6 mm) from upper and side edges. Stitch several times across bottom of side opening, to reinforce.

Log Cabin Design

Log Cabin remains one of the most popular traditional designs. The instructions that follow use chainstitching for quick and easy piecing of multiple blocks.

Choose three fabrics for each half of the block, and a fabric for the center square. Fabrics may graduate from light to dark, or from dark to light on each side of the center square, or they may be arranged in a random order.

The instructions that follow make a 7" (18 cm) finished block that is used in the sampler quilts (pages 214 and 215). A smaller Log Cabin block is used for the miniquilts (page 210).

How to Sew a Log Cabin Quilt Block

1) Cut 1½" (3.8 cm) strips across the width of seven different fabrics. Label strips from A to G, as shown.

2) Stitch Strips A and B, right sides together, along one long side. Press seam allowances away from strip A. Cut across the pieced strip at 1½" (3.8 cm) intervals.

3) Stitch pieced units to a second Strip B, using chainstitching (page 40) as shown.

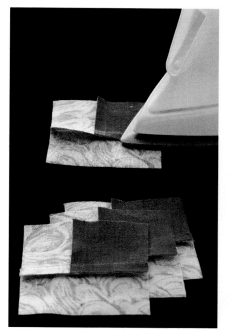

4) Trim Strip B even with edges of pieced units. Press seam allowances away from center squares.

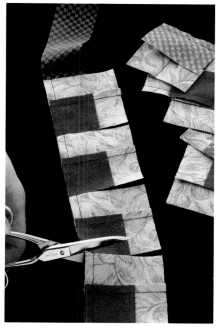

5) Stitch three-piece units to Strip C, using chainstitching; position units at 90° angle to most recent seam on side nearest center square. Trim Strip C even with edges of pieced units. Press seam allowances away from center squares.

6) Stitch four-piece units to a second Strip C, using chainstitching; position units at 90° angle to the most recent seam on side nearest center square. Continue in this manner, stitching two strips of each color to pieced units in sequence. Press the seam allowances away from center square.

Log Cabin Miniquilts

This trio of quilts, made using the Log Cabin design (page 208), creates a stunning wall display. The blocks in each quilt are arranged in a different way to create three different designs.

For a subtle blending of colors with a contemporary feel, make the blocks using hand-dyed fabrics as shown in the quilts opposite. These solid-colored fabrics are available in packets of six or eight fabrics and can be purchased from quilting stores and mail-order suppliers. Choose a printed fabric for the border, binding, and center square of the quilt blocks.

The quilts can also be made using a combination of printed fabrics. For best results, select fabrics for one half of the block that contrast with the fabrics for the other half. This emphasizes the design created by the block arrangement.

The quilts are made from 3½" (9 cm) blocks. Each of the finished quilts measures about 18" × 25" (46 × 63.5 cm). The yardages and the cutting instructions below are for a set of three quilts.

✄ Cutting Directions

Label the fabrics for the block design as on page 212, steps 1a or 1b. Cut the following strips across the width of the fabric: seven 1" (2.5 cm) strips each, from Fabrics B and C; eleven 1" (2.5 cm) strips each, from Fabrics D and E; and sixteen 1" (2.5 cm) strips each, from Fabrics F and G.

Cut two 1" (2.5 cm) strips from the fabric for the center squares of the blocks; these are Strips A.

Cut six 2½" (6.5 cm) strips from the fabric for the border; the strips will be cut to length as on page 212, steps 4 and 5.

YOU WILL NEED

½-yd. (0.5 m) bundle of six hand-dyed fabrics in a light to dark gradation; or ½ yd. (0.5 m) each of three light and three dark printed fabrics.

1 yd. (0.95 m) fabric, for borders and center square of each block.

½ yd. (0.5 m) fabric, for binding.

1⅞ yd. (1.75 m) fabric, for backing.

Batting, three pieces, about 22" × 29" (56 × 73.5 cm) each.

Log Cabin quilt blocks can be made from either solid-colored or printed fabrics and sewn into three design arrangements to make the miniquilts opposite.

How to Sew a Log Cabin Miniquilt

1a) Hand-dyed fabrics. Arrange and label six hand-dyed fabrics from B to G, graduating from dark to light and light to dark as indicated. Fabric for center square is Fabric A.

1b) Printed fabrics. Determine the arrangement of the fabrics, cutting narrow strips, if necessary; position three light fabrics on one half of the block and three dark fabrics on the other half. Label fabrics from A to G as indicated.

2) Assemble 72 Log Cabin blocks as on page 209, steps 2 to 6; in step 2, cut across pieced strip at 1" (2.5 cm) intervals.

3) Arrange blocks four across and six down, as shown in the quilts on pages 210 and 211.

4) Stitch the blocks into rows; stitch rows together, finger-pressing seam allowances in opposite directions. Press quilt top. Measure each quilt top across the middle; determine shortest measurement.

5) Layer fabric strips for borders and cut six strips to measurement determined in step 4 for upper and lower borders; remainder of border strips will be trimmed to size for side borders on page 213, step 6.

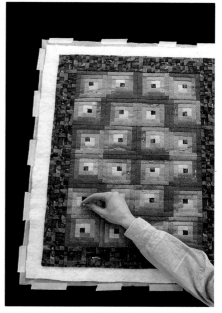

6) Stitch upper and lower border strips to each quilt top as on page 164, step 10. Measure each quilt top down the middle, including border strips; determine shortest measurement. From remaining border strips, cut six side borders to this length.

7) Stitch border strips to sides of each quilt top. Press seam allowances toward borders. Press quilt top.

8) Cut backing fabric for each quilt 4" (10 cm) wider and longer than quilt top. Layer and baste the quilt top, batting, and backing (pages 96 to 99).

9) Quilt wall hangings, using stitch-in-the-ditch method (pages 104 and 105), stitching in seamlines joining blocks and borders. Stitch additional diagonal lines through centers of blocks to accentuate design as indicated by arrows. Apply binding to quilts as on pages 112 and 113. Attach fabric sleeve to each quilt (page 165).

Sampler Quilt

Sampler quilts are made from a variety of quilt blocks, united through color and size. The instructions that follow are for a 56" × 77" (142 × 195.5 cm) sampler quilt that can be used as a wall hanging, lap quilt, or twin-size bed quilt. Although the quilt may appear complex and intricate, it is easily assembled from the nine quilt blocks, plain fabric panels, quick-pieced checkerboards, and pieced-triangle strips.

The quilt is designed with four vertical columns that are separated by sashing strips. A narrow inner border frames the quilt, and Log Cabin blocks form a colorful outer border.

This sampler quilt is an attractive way to showcase a variety of quilting techniques. The example shown opposite has template quilting on the sashing strips, and the plain fabric blocks are embellished with free-motion stipple quilting, motif quilting, and template quilting.

Sampler quilts can be made using several fabrics, sometimes even as many as thirty. To simplify fabric selection, start with two or three multicolored fabrics to set the theme. Use the theme fabrics for the plain fabric panels; then incorporate them in some of the pieced blocks. The theme fabrics set the overall tone of the quilt. When choosing theme fabrics, think about scale. A larger print with many colors makes it easier to select the remaining fabrics.

Choose fabric colors with values that range from light to dark. Select a variety of fabrics, including solids, prints, checks, and stripes. You may want to keep swatches in a notebook and collect fabrics over a period of time. Multicolored prints work especially well when making the pieced checkerboard strips. Solid-colored fabrics are used for the sashing strips to separate and define the columns and the border of the quilt.

When piecing the quilt top, it is important to stitch scant ¼" (6 mm) seams. This allows for shrinkage resulting from multiple stitched seams and ensures that the pieced border will fit around the quilt top.

Sampler quilt (opposite) incorporates nine quilt block designs and a variety of quilting techniques.

✂ Cutting Directions

For Column One of the sampler quilt, cut one 7½" × 12½" (19.3 × 31.8 cm) rectangle and one 6½" × 12½" (16.3 × 31.8 cm) rectangle from theme fabric for the plain fabric panels.

For Column Two, cut one 6½" × 8½" (16.3 × 21.8 cm) rectangle, one 6½" × 9½" (16.3 × 24.3 cm) rectangle, and one 6½" × 11" (16.3 × 28 cm) rectangle from theme fabric for the plain fabric panels.

For Column Three, cut one 9½" × 10" (24.3 × 25.5 cm) rectangle and one 9½" × 11" (24.3 × 28 cm) rectangle from theme fabric for the plain fabric panels.

For Column Four, cut one 6½" × 10½" (16.3 × 27.8 cm) rectangle, and one 6½" × 12½" (16.3 × 31.8 cm) rectangle from theme fabric for the plain fabric panels.

For the pieced blocks and pieced strips, cut the fabrics as on pages 218 to 223.

For the vertical sashing strips, cut fabric strips across the width of the fabric. Cut two 3½" (9 cm) strips from first sashing fabric, to join Columns One and Two. Cut two 2½" (6.5 cm) strips from second sashing fabric, to join Columns Two and Three. Cut two 2½" (6.5 cm) strips from third sashing fabric, to join Columns Three and Four.

For the inner plain border, cut six 1½" (3.8 cm) strips across the width of the fabric. For the outer Log Cabin border, cut 1½" (3.8 cm) strips across the width of seven fabrics. Light-colored fabrics may be used for one half of the block and dark-colored fabrics for the other half. Cut the number of fabric strips as follows:
Fabric A, two strips for center squares;
Fabric B, four inner light strips;
Fabric C, six inner dark strips;
Fabric D, eight middle light strips;
Fabric E, ten middle dark strips;
Fabric F, eleven outer light strips; and
Fabric G, thirteen outer dark strips.

For the binding, cut seven 2½" (6.5 cm) strips.

YOU WILL NEED

Two or three multicolored theme fabrics.
Assorted fabrics, for pieced blocks and pieced strips.
¼ **yd. (0.25 m) each of three fabrics,** for vertical sashing strips.
⅓ **yd. (0.32 m) fabric,** for inner border.
Fabrics for Log Cabin border: ⅛ yd. (0.15 m) Fabric A, ¼ yd. (0.25 m) Fabric B, ⅜ yd. (0.35 m) Fabric C, ⅜ yd. (0.35 m) Fabric D, ½ yd. (0.5 m) Fabric E, ½ yd. (0.5 m) Fabric F, ⅝ yd. (0.6 m) Fabric G.
Batting, about 60" × 81" (152.5 × 206 cm).
3½ **yd. (3.2 m) fabric,** for backing.
⅝ **yd. (0.6 m) fabric,** for binding.

Diagram of the Sampler Quilt

Color-coded Identification Chart
for the Diagram of the Sampler Quilt

Log Cabin blocks	
Ohio Star blocks	
Pieced-triangle strips	
Checkerboard strips	
Theme fabrics (choose two or three)	
Shadowed Square blocks	
Drunkard's Path units	
Pieced Heart blocks	
Card Trick blocks	
Double Nine-patch block	
Spools block	
Nine-patch block	
Sashing strips (choose three)	
Inner border	
Binding	

How to Sew Column One of the Sampler Quilt

1) Sew one 12" (30.5 cm) block each of the following: Ohio Star (page 166), Drunkard's Path (page 172), and Shadowed Square (page 190). Set aside two of the remaining strip-pieced triangles from the Shadowed Square design for use in Column Two.

2) Cut two 6⅞" (17.5 cm) squares each from two fabrics for pieced-triangle strips. Layer squares and cut once diagonally. Stitch one triangle from each fabric, right sides together, along long edge. Finger-press seam allowances to one side; trim points. Repeat with remaining triangles to make four squares.

3) Stitch two pieced squares right sides together as shown, to make a pieced-triangle strip. Finger-press seam allowances to one side. Repeat to make a second pieced-triangle strip for Column Four; set aside.

4) Cut two 1½" × 20" (3.8 × 51 cm) strips each from two fabrics. Stitch strips together lengthwise, alternating fabrics, to make a 4½" × 20" (11.5 × 51 cm) pieced strip. Press seam allowances in one direction.

5) Trim short end of pieced strip at 90° angle. Cut twelve 1½" (3.8 cm) strips across the pieced strip. Stitch pieced strips together, alternating fabrics to make a 4½" × 12½" (11.5 × 31.8 cm) checkerboard strip.

6) Cut one 1½" × 20" (3.8 × 51 cm) strip from each of two fabrics; make a 2½" × 12½" (6.5 × 31.8 cm) checkerboard strip as in steps 4 and 5.

7) Stitch blocks, checkerboard strips, pieced-triangle strip, and the theme-fabric rectangles into a column as desired. Press the pieced column, pressing seam allowances in one direction.

How to Sew Column Two of the Sampler Quilt

1) Make one 6" (15 cm) Pieced Heart block (page 158); set aside the remaining heart units for use in Column Four. Using the strip-pieced triangles set aside from Column One, make two Shadowed Square blocks as on page 191, steps 4 and 5; in step 4, cut one 6⅞" (17.5 cm) square. Stitch blocks together as shown to make a vertical strip.

2) Cut one 7" (18 cm) square each from two fabrics. Using circle template with 5" (12.5 cm) diameter, cut one circle each from two fabrics, adding scant ¼" (6 mm) seam allowance. Continue to make a total of eight Drunkard's Path units as on page 173, steps 3 to 6.

3) Arrange four Drunkard's Path units as shown. Stitch units together to form two rows; stitch rows together. Set aside remaining units for use in Column Four.

4) Cut three 1½" × 11" (3.8 × 28 cm) strips from each of two fabrics. Continue as on page 201, center, steps 2 and 3; in step 2, press seam allowances in one direction, and, in step 3, cut six strips across each pieced strip. Stitch strips together, alternating fabrics to make two 3½" × 6½" (9 × 16.3 cm) checkerboard strips.

5) Cut two 2⅞" (7.2 cm) squares from two fabrics for pieced-triangle strip; cut the squares in half once diagonally. Stitch one triangle from each fabric, right sides together, along long edge. Repeat with the remaining triangles to make three pieced-triangle squares.

6) Stitch the pieced-triangle squares together, side by side, to make a 2½" × 6½" (6.5 × 16.3 cm) strip. Finger-press seam allowances to one side.

7) Stitch blocks, checkerboard strips, pieced-triangle strip, and theme-fabric rectangles into a column as desired. Press the pieced column, pressing the seam allowances in one direction.

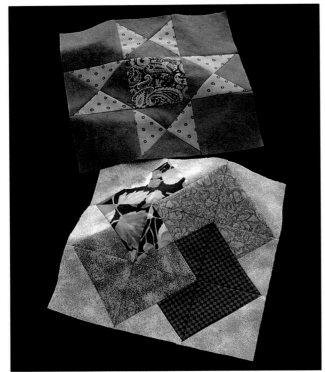

1) Make one 9" (23 cm) Ohio Star block (page 166) and one 9" (23 cm) Card Trick block (page 178).

2) Make one 9" (23 cm) Spools block (page 184) and one Double Nine-patch block (page 200).

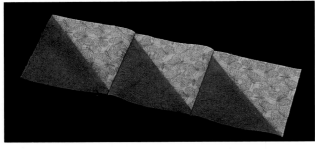

3) Cut two 3⅞" (9.7 cm) squares from each of two fabrics for pieced-triangle strip. Make a 3½" × 9½" (9 × 24.3 cm) strip as on page 219, steps 5 and 6; in step 5, omit reference to 2⅞" (7.2 cm) squares.

4) Cut one 1½" × 15½" (3.8 × 39.3 cm) strip each from two fabrics. Make 2½" × 9½" (6.5 × 24.3 cm) checkerboard strip as on page 218, steps 4 and 5; in step 5, cut nine strips across pieced strip.

5) Stitch blocks, checkerboard strip, pieced-triangle strip, and theme-fabric rectangles into a column as desired. Press pieced column, pressing seam allowances in one direction.

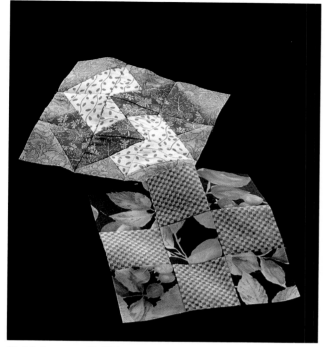

1) Make one 6" (15 cm) Card Trick block (page 178) and one 6" (15 cm) Nine-patch block (page 200).

2) Stitch two remaining Drunkard's Path units from Column Two together as shown to make a two-patch block; discard remaining units. Complete second 6" (15 cm) Pieced Heart block from units remaining from Column Two.

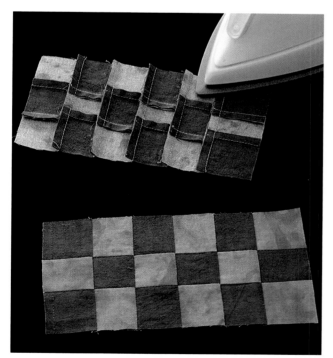

3) Make two 3½" × 6½" (9 × 16.3 cm) checkerboard strips as on page 219, step 4.

4) Stitch blocks, pieced-triangle strip, checkerboard strips, two-patch Drunkard's Path block, and theme-fabric rectangles into a column as desired. Press pieced column, pressing seam allowances in one direction. Assemble quilt as on pages 222 and 223.

How to Assemble the Sampler Quilt

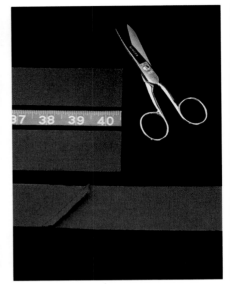

1) Stitch short ends of corresponding vertical sashing strips together. Trim the seam allowances; finger-press to one side. Trim each sashing strip to measure 61½" (156.3 cm).

2) Mark centers of vertical sashing strips and columns. Pin one sashing strip to one column, right sides together, matching the centers and ends. Pin along length, easing in any excess fullness; stitch. Repeat to join all sashing strips and columns. Press the seam allowances toward sashing.

3) Stitch short ends of two strips for inner border together. Trim the seam allowances; finger-press to one side. Repeat to make a second pieced strip. Trim pieced strips to 63½" (161.3 cm), for side strips of inner border. Trim remaining strips to 40½" (103 cm), for upper and lower strips of inner border.

4) Pin inner border strip to upper edge of the quilt top at the center and ends, right sides together; pin along length, easing in any fullness. Stitch; press the seam allowances toward the inner border. Repeat at lower edge.

5) Pin and stitch pieced strips to sides of quilt top as in step 4. Press seam allowances toward the inner border.

6) Assemble 34 Log Cabin blocks, as on page 209, steps 2 to 6. Stitch six Log Cabin blocks together for the upper border strip, placing the color values as shown in diagram on page 216. Finger-press the seam allowances to one side. Repeat to stitch strip for lower edge.

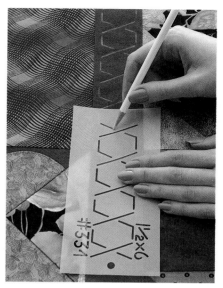

7) Pin the light-colored side of Log Cabin strip to upper edge of quilt top at center and ends, right sides together; pin along length, easing in any fullness. Stitch; press seam allowances toward the inner border. Repeat at lower edge.

8) Stitch 11 Log Cabin blocks together for the side border strip, placing the color values as shown in the diagram on page 216. Repeat for remaining side strip. Pin and stitch pieced strips to sides of quilt top as in step 7. Press the seam allowances toward the border.

9) Mark quilting lines for template quilting as desired (page 102). Cut backing 4" (10 cm) wider and longer than quilt top, piecing the fabric as necessary. Layer and baste quilt top, batting, and backing (pages 96 to 99).

10) Quilt along sashing and inner border as on pages 104 and 105, using the stitch-in-the-ditch method; then complete free-motion and template quilting within the theme fabrics and sashing strips as on pages 104 to 106.

11) Stitch in the ditch along seams of pieced blocks as on pages 104 and 105. Stitch in the ditch between the Log Cabin blocks, and stitch through blocks diagonally in both directions, making an X; use continuous stitching, and pivot the stitching ¼" (6 mm) from raw edge at seams between blocks. Apply binding as on pages 112 and 113.

Quilted Garments
& Accessories

Drunkard's Path Vests

Hand-dyed quilt fabrics and the raw edge appliqué technique are combined in this vest for color and texture. The vest is made using the Drunkard's Path design on page 172. As shown opposite and in the instructions that follow, a graduated effect is achieved by using fabrics that range from light to dark. Other color arrangements may be used for different effects.

Piece and quilt the outer fabric before cutting out the garment. For a lightweight vest without bulk, use a thin batting designed for quilted garments. Or use cotton flannel in place of batting. When using cotton flannel, be sure to prewash the fabric to help prevent shrinkage in the finished garment.

The Drunkard's Path units used in this project are constructed using a method similar to that on pages 172 and 173; however, it is not necessary to press under the edges of the circles. The circles are simply cut and stitched to the background square, allowing the raw edges to fray slightly.

Select a commercial pattern for a lined, loose-fitting vest. Avoid fitted vests, because the darts and the additional seams would interrupt the design of the pieced fabric.

✂ Cutting Directions

Cut two vest fronts and one vest back from lining, using the commercial pattern. The Drunkard's Path units for the pieced yardage are cut and assembled on pages 228 and 229. The vest fronts and vest back are cut from the pieced fabric and batting or flannel on page 229, step 10.

YOU WILL NEED

Commercial pattern, for lined, loose-fitting vest.

¼-yd. (0.25 m) bundle of hand-dyed fabrics, for circles; or ¼ yd. (0.25 m) each of several fabrics as desired.

Fabric for background, yardage indicated on pattern plus ¼ yd. (0.25 m).

Lining fabric; yardage indicated on pattern.

Thin batting, such as Thermore®, or prewashed cotton flannel.

Tear-away stabilizer.

How to Sew a Drunkard's Path Vest

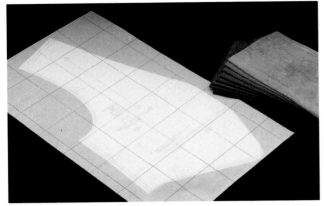

1) Measure vest fronts and vest back, and determine the number of 3" (7.5 cm) Drunkard's Path units that are needed for each piece; units extend beyond cutting lines. Estimate the number of units needed of each color; you need one circle for every four units.

2) Cut a 5" (12.5 cm) circle from heavy cardboard or template material. Using template and pencil, trace template design onto fabric; cut out circles.

3) Cut 7" (18 cm) squares from background fabric, cutting one square for every four Drunkard's Path units. Center one fabric circle on background square, matching grainlines. Position tear-away stabilizer, cut larger than circle, on wrong side of background square; pin circle in place. Repeat for remaining circles.

4) Stitch around fabric circle, ⅛" to ³⁄₁₆" (3 to 4.5 mm) from raw edge, using short stitch length. Repeat for remaining circles. Remove tear-away stabilizer, taking care not to distort stitches.

5) Cut through squares in both directions to make four Drunkard's Path units.

6) Arrange Drunkard's Path units for right and left vest front as shown, making sure the two sections are mirror images.

7) Stitch units into rows; then stitch the rows together, finger-pressing seam allowances in opposite directions. Press pieced sections.

8) Arrange Drunkard's Path units for vest back as shown. Stitch the units into rows; then stitch the rows together, finger-pressing seam allowances in opposite directions. Press pieced section.

9) Cut batting to size for each pieced section. Place the pieced sections over batting; baste with thread or safety pins. Quilt, using stitch-in-the-ditch method (pages 104 and 105), in seamlines of pieced units.

10) Cut two vest fronts and one vest back from quilted fabric sections, taking care to match quilted design at side seams. You may want to cut one vest front and turn the piece over, to use as the pattern for cutting the remaining vest front.

11) Complete vest, following pattern instructions; eliminate any interfacing from vest. Press vest from lining side to avoid shiny areas over seam allowances.

12) Brush edges of appliqués, using a stiff brush; this ravels the edges for more texture.

Pieced Vests with Triangle Squares

Triangle designs and a variety of quilting techniques give this vest its unique look. The left side of the vest features a pieced triangle strip. To balance the design, the right side of the vest has folded triangles of fabric, called prairie points, inserted into a diagonal seam. A pocket on the right side of the vest gives added detail. The lined vest is constructed using a low-loft batting. This provides the quilting dimension while adding minimal bulk.

Select a commercial pattern for a lined vest without darts. Because the fabric is quilted after the vest is constructed, choose a vest that is loose fitting; the quilting will cause the garment to shrink up in size slightly.

✂ Cutting Directions

Cut two vest fronts and one vest back each from the lining fabric and batting, using the commercial pattern pieces. The pieced outer vest is cut during construction.

For the pieced-triangle strip, cut one 3½" (9 cm) strip each from two or more fabrics, cutting across the width of the fabric; use at least one solid-colored fabric. Cut the strips to make 3½" (9 cm) squares; then cut the squares once diagonally to make triangles.

For the prarie points, cut three to five 4" (10 cm) squares from fabric.

YOU WILL NEED

Commercial pattern, for lined, loose-fitting vest.

Four or five coordinating prints, about ½ yd. (0.5 m) each.

Scraps of solid-colored fabrics, for pieced-triangle strip, prairie points, and trim on pocket.

Lining fabric, yardage as indicated on pattern.

Low-loft batting, yardage as indicated for lining.

Scrap of thin batting, such as Thermore®, or prewashed cotton flannel, for pocket batting.

How to Make the Pattern for a Pieced Vest with Triangle Squares

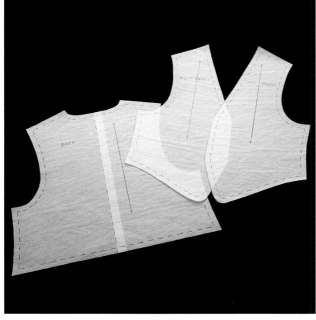

1) Trace pattern front, including seamlines on paper; turn pattern over, and repeat. Label pieces as right front and left front; mark grainlines. Trace pattern back, including seamlines on paper; turn the pattern over, and repeat. Tape the back pieces together along the center back seam. Label as pattern back. Cut the patterns on marked lines.

2) Mark a horizontal seamline on right front pattern, about 6" to 8" (15 to 20.5 cm) from the lower edge of the pattern; this line is also for the upper edge of the pocket. Mark a vertical line through the lower section; label lower right section as pocket area.

(Continued on next page)

How to Make the Pattern for a Pieced Vest with Triangle Squares (continued)

3) Trace the pocket area to make pocket pattern. Add ¼" (6 mm) seam allowance on inner edge as shown. Do not add seam allowance at upper edge. Mark grainline.

4) Mark a diagonal line through the upper right section, from edge of armhole to front edge; line at front edge should be at least ½" (1.3 cm) above the horizontal line. This is the seamline for inserting prairie points.

5) Mark a horizontal seamline on left front pattern, about 4" (10 cm) below shoulder seam. For the pieced-triangle strip, mark lower section with a vertical section, 5¼" (13.2 cm) wide, as shown; mark lines parallel to grainline.

6) Mark a horizontal yoke seamline on vest back; mark line perpendicular to grainline. Divide lower section of pattern into three or more sections as desired, using straight or angled lines. Mark notches on all front and back pieces along new seamlines to indicate where vest sections are to be matched.

7) Trace the pattern sections for front and back on paper, adding ¼" (6 mm) seam allowances to inner seamlines. Mark grainlines on each section. Number the original pattern sections and traced sections to correspond. Cut pattern sections.

232

How to Sew a Pieced Vest with Triangle Squares

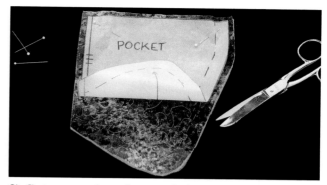

1) Make pattern, opposite. Set aside pattern sections for pocket and pieced-triangle strip. Using sections for vest fronts and vest back, cut one piece each from fabric as desired.

2) Cut one pocket piece each from the outer pocket fabric, thin batting or flannel, and the backing fabric, cutting pieces slightly larger than the pocket pattern. Layer fabrics; baste around the outer edges. Quilt as desired (pages 100 to 108). Cut pocket, using pattern. (Contrasting thread was used to show detail.)

3) Cut a 2½" (6.5 cm) bias fabric strip, with length of strip slightly longer than width of pocket. Press under ¼" (6 mm) on one long edge. Pin opposite edge of strip to upper edge of pocket, right sides together. Stitch ¼" (6 mm) seam.

4) Fold bias strip to wrong side of pocket, creating ¼" (6 mm) binding on right side; stitch in the ditch on right side of pocket. Slipstitch folded edge of the strip to the wrong side of pocket.

5) Pin pocket to the corresponding vest piece, labeled pocket area, matching raw edges at sides and lower edge; baste in place. Stitch pocket section to remaining lower section of right vest front.

6) Fold each fabric square for prairie points in half lengthwise; press. Fold sides as shown, to make a triangle; press.

7) Position prairie points on upper section of right vest front, overlapping triangles as desired; folded edges may face either up or down. Pin triangles in place. Machine-baste in place a scant ¼" (6 mm) from raw edges.

(Continued on next page)

How to Sew a Pieced Vest with Triangle Squares (continued)

8) Stitch the upper right and middle right sections together, matching notches; press seam allowances to one side. Stitch upper pieced section to lower pieced section; press.

9) Stitch two different triangles for pieced-triangle strip, right sides together, along long edge; finger-press seam allowances to one side. Repeat to make about 14 pieced-triangle squares.

10) Arrange triangle squares, two across, in desired arrangement for the pieced-triangle strip. Make any additional triangle squares as necessary for required length or color arrangement. Stitch the squares into rows; then stitch rows together, finger-pressing seam allowances in opposite directions. Press.

11) Cut pieced-triangle strip to size, using pattern set aside in step 1.

12) Stitch pieced-triangle strip to side sections of left front, in 1/4" (6 mm) seams; press seam allowances away from the strip. Stitch lower pieced section to upper left section; press the seam allowances toward the shoulder seam.

13) Stitch together lower sections of vest back in 1/4" (6 mm) seams, matching notches; press the seam allowances to one side. Stitch lower section to back yoke; press seam allowances toward yoke.

14) Place each outer vest piece over corresponding batting piece; pin in place, using safety pins. Baste batting to outer vest pieces, 1/2" (1.3 cm) from raw edges.

15) Stitch shoulder seams of front and back outer vest together; repeat for lining. Trim batting seam allowances of outer vest.

16) Pin the outer vest and lining right sides together, matching raw edges. Stitch around outer edges; do not stitch the side seams. Trim the batting and seam allowances.

17) Turn vest right side out through side openings of vest; lightly press edges. Pin-baste the layers together, using safety pins.

18) Quilt the vest (pages 100 to 108), changing quilting techniques as desired for each fabric section; do not extend stitching into seam allowances at side seams.

19) Stitch ⅝" (1.5 cm) side seams, with right sides together. Trim the seam allowances of the vest front to ⅛" (3 mm); trim the remaining batting seam allowance close to stitching.

20) Turn under ¼" (6 mm) on the raw edges of the untrimmed seam allowances; pin, enclosing narrow trimmed edge. Hand-stitch folded edge to vest front lining. Hand-stitch the prairie points to the vest front, if desired.

Pieced-triangle Jackets

Make a quilted shawl-collar jacket using fabric pieced from equilateral triangles. A low-loft polyester batting is used to give the jacket loft and warmth. The outer edges of the jacket are trimmed with bias binding for contrast. Buttons are used to secure the layers together, adding extra detail and eliminating the need for machine quilting.

The 6" (15 cm) equilateral triangles can be cut quickly using a quilter's tool, such as the Easy Three™. Or they can be cut using a cardboard template. Piece the triangles randomly to make fabric yardage slightly larger than each pattern piece.

Choose a commercial pattern for a lined shawl-collar jacket that is loose fitting and has rounded lower corners at the center front. The loft of the batting will take up some of the design ease, making the jacket fit a little closer. Purchase yardage for the outer jacket to equal the total yardage indicated on the pattern plus ¾ yd. to 1 yd. (0.7 to 0.95 m) to allow for the seam allowances of the piecing. For example, if the yardage requirement is 4⅛ yd. (3.8 m), you may want to purchase 1 yd. (0.95 m) each of five different fabrics. For a coordinated look, purchase additional yardage of two of the fabrics to use for the jacket lining and binding.

To construct the jacket, the upper collar and front facing pieces are cut from the lining and stitched to the lining pieces to make a separate inner jacket. The batting is basted to the outer jacket only. When pinning the outer jacket pieces to the batting, you can prevent the batting from shifting by laying the batting on a carpeted floor or by taping the batting to the surface of a table. After basting, the inner jacket and outer jacket are stitched together and the outer edges are finished with bias binding.

✂ Cutting Directions

Cut 5¾" (14.5 cm) strips across the width of the fabrics for the outer jacket. Cut the strips into triangles, below, using the quilter's tool or template.

Adjust the pattern pieces as on page 238, steps 1 and 2. From the lining fabric, cut the front lining pieces, back lining pieces, sleeves, and the upper collar and front facing pieces.

For the binding, cut 3¼" (8.2 cm) bias strips.

YOU WILL NEED

Commercial pattern for shawl-collar jacket, selected according to the guidelines at left.
1 yd. (0.95 m) each of five or more fabrics, for pieced outer jacket.
Lining fabric, yardage as indicated on pattern; extra yardage may be required for cutting the upper collar and facing.
¾ yd. (0.7 m) fabric, for binding.
Low-loft polyester batting in twin bed size.
Buttons.

How to Cut Equilateral Triangles

Quilter's tool. Align Easy Three tool with fabric strip at the marking for 6" (15 cm) equilateral triangle; cut along angled edge of tool. Turn tool over, and realign with edge of fabric strip at marking for 6" (15 cm) triangle; cut along the angled edge. Repeat to cut triangles from all the fabric strips.

Template. 1) Mark a 6" (15 cm) line on cardboard or plastic template material. From center of this line, mark a perpendicular line. Align end of ruler to end of first line, and rotate ruler until 6" (15 cm) mark meets perpendicular line; draw line. Repeat for remaining side of triangle. Add ¼" (6 mm) seam allowances.

2) Cut template on marked lines. Align template with raw edges of fabric strips, allowing tip of triangle to extend on one side. Mark along angled sides, using marking pencil. Rotate and realign the template to mark the second triangle. Repeat to mark triangles on all the fabric strips. Cut on the marked lines.

How to Sew a Pieced-triangle Jacket

1) Trim seam allowances from center front of pattern for outer jacket, and on outer edges of the upper and undercollar pattern pieces. Trim the lower edge of front, back, and sleeve pattern pieces along foldlines for hems.

2) Align outer front pattern to front lining pattern. Trim lower edge of front lining pattern even with lower edge of outer front pattern. Repeat for outer back pattern and back lining pattern. Eliminate any center back pleat and any back neck facing on back lining pieces. Set aside sleeve lining pattern piece; sleeve lining is cut from outer sleeve pattern.

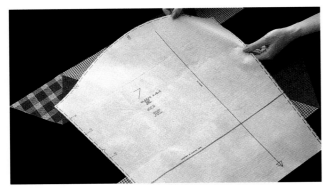

3) Stitch the triangles into rows, taking care not to stretch bias edges; position straight-of-grain edges of triangles along upper and lower edges of rows. Press seam allowances to one side. Rows for each garment section should be slightly wider than corresponding pattern piece.

4) Stitch rows together, aligning points; make sections of pieced fabric slightly longer than pattern pieces.

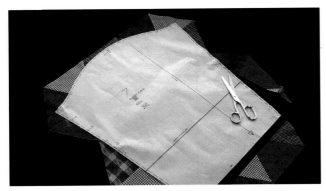

5) Cut jacket fronts, back, and sleeves from pieced fabric sections. Undercollar can be cut from pieced fabric or from plain fabric.

6) Position the outer jacket pieces and undercollar on batting; do not use upper collar and front facing pieces. Pin fabric to batting, using straight pins along edges of fabric and safety pins within the pieces. Cut batting even with edges of jacket pieces. Machine-baste layers together a scant ½" (1.3 cm) from raw edges.

7) Assemble outer jacket, following pattern instructions; upper collar and front facing are stitched to lining in step 9. Place tissue paper strips against batting to prevent catching on presser foot and feed dogs. Trim batting from seam allowances.

8) Assemble and apply the patch pockets to jacket fronts, if included with pattern, following the pattern instructions; reinforce pocket piece with interfacing, if desired.

9) Staystitch the neck edge of back lining; clip to stitching. Stitch the upper collar and front facing to the front lining; then stitch to the back lining along the shoulder and neck seams, pivoting at the corners at neck edge.

10) Place lining inside jacket, wrong sides together, aligning seams; pin along edges. Stitch scant ½" (1.3 cm) seams around outer edges of jacket and lower edges of sleeves.

11) Stitch binding strips together; trim. Press binding in half, wrong sides together. Starting near side seam of jacket, stitch binding to jacket, with right sides together and raw edges even, ½" (1.3 cm) from raw edges; fold back ½" (1.3 cm) at beginning of strip, and overlap ends about ¾" (2 cm).

12) Wrap binding to inside of jacket. Stitch in the ditch, or hand-stitch binding in place. Apply binding to sleeves.

13) Quilt the jacket by securing buttons at points of triangles, stitching through all layers. Follow pattern directions for button and buttonhole closure.

Tote Bags

This generously sized tote bag is a handy carry-all for all ages. A center panel displays two quilt blocks on each side of the bag. To make a tote bag for carrying sewing supplies, use the Spools design on page 184 for the center insert. Or use the Double Nine-patch design on page 200 to make a tote bag that coordinates with the sleeping bag on page 203.

The lined bag has an inside pocket that is secured with hook and loop tape. Webbing is used to create sturdy handles for the bag and to trim the sides of the center panel.

For the efficient use of fabric, the side panels are cut on the crosswise grain. For this reason, select a nondirectional print.

✂ Cutting Directions

Cut two 6¾" × 39½" (17 × 100.3 cm) rectangles from the fabric for the side panels; also cut one 3½" × 9½" (9 × 24.3 cm) rectangle for the bottom of the center panel. From the lining fabric, cut one 22" × 39½" (56 × 100.3 cm) rectangle; also cut two 8½" (21.8 cm) squares, for the pocket.

YOU WILL NEED

How to Sew a Spools Tote Bag

1) **Make** four Spools blocks as on pages 184 to 186. Stitch lower edge of one block to the upper edge of second block, to make the center panel for front. Repeat for back center panel.

2) **Pin** front center panel to bottom piece, right sides together, matching 9½" (24.3 cm) edges; stitch ¼" (6 mm) seam. Repeat for back panel. Press the seam allowances toward bottom of bag.

(Continued on next page)

How to Sew a Spools Tote Bag (continued)

3) Pin side panels to center panel, with right sides together and raw edges even. Stitch scant ¼" (6 mm) seams. Press the seam allowances toward sides of bag.

4) Layer and baste the outer bag, batting, and inner lining (pages 96 to 99). Quilt (pages 100 to 108); use stitch-in-the-ditch method on quilt blocks and stipple quilting, channel quilting, or template quilting on side panels.

5) Trim the batting and inner lining even with edges of outer bag. Layer the quilted outer fabric over lining; trim lining to match.

6) Fold webbing in half; pin-mark. Stitch ends of webbing together in ½" (1.3 cm) seam; press open. Topstitch scant ¼" (6 mm) from seam on each side. Trim seam to ¼" (6 mm).

7) Glue-baste wrong side of strap to right side of bag, overlapping edge of webbing ⅛" (3 mm) over center panel; center the seam and the pin mark on strap on bottom of bag.

8) Topstitch along both sides of the webbing; begin and end stitching 1¼" (3.2 cm) from the upper edges of the bag.

9) Fold bag in half crosswise, right sides together. Stitch ¼" (6 mm) seams on sides.

10) Stitch pocket pieces, right sides together, around all four sides, stitching ¼" (6 mm) from edges and leaving an opening along one side for turning. Turn pocket right side out. Cut 7¼" (18.7 cm) length of hook and loop tape. Center hook side of tape along upper edge of pocket; stitch in place.

11) Center the pocket on lining, 4" (10 cm) from one short edge. Mark position for loop side of tape; stitch to lining. Reposition the pocket on lining; pin. Edgestitch around sides and lower edge.

12) Fold bag lining in half crosswise, with right sides together. Stitch ¼" (6 mm) seams on sides, leaving 6" (15 cm) opening in one seam.

13) Insert outer bag inside lining, right sides together. Pin along upper edges, matching side seams; finger-press seam allowances of bag and lining in opposite directions. Stitch ¼" (6 mm) seam at upper edge; do not catch webbing in stitching.

14) Turn bag right side out through the opening in side seam of lining; machine-stitch opening closed. Press upper edge of bag.

15) Turn outer bag inside lining; align side seams. Mark a 3" (7.5 cm) line across corners. Stitch on line, through outer bag and lining.

16) Edgestitch along upper edge of bag. Secure the strap to top of bag as shown, stitching an X through all layers.

How to Sew a Double Nine-patch Tote Bag

1) Make two Double Nine-patch blocks as on page 201. Make two more blocks, using four checkerboard squares and five plain squares in each block.

2) Stitch the blocks together as shown, to make front center panel and back center panel. Complete tote bag as on pages 241 to 243, steps 2 to 16.

Wallet-style Purses

This quilted purse is divided into compartments like a wallet. It is constructed with three pockets for holding coins, credit cards, and a checkbook or currency. Each pocket is secured with hook and loop tape. The wallet becomes a shoulder bag with a length of decorative cording for the strap.

Wallet-style purse has three convenient pockets: a checkbook or currency pocket in the center, with coin and credit card pockets on the sides.

✂ Cutting Directions

Cut one 6½" × 19" (16.3 × 48.5 cm) rectangle from the outer fabric. Cut one 8" × 21" (20.5 × 53.5 cm) rectangle from the backing fabric.

Cut one 5½" (14 cm) strip from lining fabric. Cut the strip to make one 5" × 5½" (12.5 × 14 cm) rectangle and one 5½" × 7½" (14 × 19.3 cm) rectangle for the coin pocket. From the strip, also cut one 5½" × 6" (14 × 15 cm) rectangle and one 5½" × 9½" (14 × 24.3 cm) rectangle for the card pocket. Trim the remaining strip length to 5½" × 8½" (14 × 21.8 cm) for the currency pocket. Also cut one rectangle 8½" × 9½" (21.8 × 24.3 cm) for the currency pocket.

Cut three 4¼" (10.8 cm) lengths and one 7¼" (18.7 cm) length of hook and loop tape.

YOU WILL NEED

¼ yd. (0.25 m) outer fabric.

½ yd. (0.5 m) lining fabric.

Heavyweight fusible interfacing.

Batting, about 8" × 21" (20.5 × 53.5 cm).

¼ yd. (0.25 m) backing fabric, such as muslin.

⅝ yd. (0.6 m) hook and loop tape, ¾" (2 cm) wide.

1½ yd. (1.4 m) decorative cording, for shoulder strap.

How to Sew a Wallet-style Purse

1) Layer outer fabric, batting, and backing; pin. Quilt as desired (pages 100 to 108). Trim the quilted piece to measure 5½" × 18" (14 × 46 cm).

2) Center short length of loop tape on one short side of quilted rectangle, ½" (1.3 cm) from the edge; this end becomes underlap of purse. Edgestitch around all four sides of tape, using zipper foot.

(Continued on next page)

How to Sew a Wallet-style Purse (continued)

3) Fold the large rectangle for coin pocket in half crosswise, matching raw edges; press. Center a short length of hook tape ¼" (6 mm) from folded edge. Edgestitch around tape.

4) Turn the folded fabric piece over; center a short length of hook tape ½" (1.3 cm) from long raw edge. Edgestitch around tape.

5) Position folded fabric piece over remaining coin pocket piece as shown, aligning the raw edges. Mark position for loop tape on bottom piece.

6) Stitch loop tape in place. Baste the pocket pieces together, a scant ¼" (6 mm) from raw edges.

7) Assemble credit card pocket following steps 3, 5, and 6 for coin pocket.

8) Place credit card pocket and outer purse piece, right sides together, at end of purse with loop tape; pin. Position coin pocket at opposite end of purse, right sides together; pin. Stitch ¼" (6 mm) from raw edges on all four sides.

9) Trim corners diagonally. Turn purse right side out. Press lightly, pressing ¼" (6 mm) seam allowances at center area of purse to the inside.

10) Fold large rectangle for currency pocket in half lengthwise; press. Center long length of hook tape ¼" (6 mm) from folded edge; edgestitch around the tape. Align the folded piece to remaining currency pocket piece; mark position for loop tape. Continue as in step 6, opposite.

11) Place currency pocket over piece of heavyweight fusible interfacing, right sides together. Stitch around all sides ¼" (6 mm) from raw edges.

12) Trim corners. Cut a slit in interfacing; turn the pocket right side out through opening. Press pocket, fusing interfacing to back of pocket.

13) Center currency pocket on inside of purse, with ends of pocket about ⅞" (2.2 cm) from folded edge of adjacent pockets. Insert ends of cording under currency pocket, at upper edge of purse, as shown; glue-baste in place.

14) Edgestitch around currency pocket. Turn to right side; edgestitch the front flaps, reinforcing the stitching at cording.

Pieced Heart Baby Bunting

This quilted bunting makes a perfect baby gift. It has a pieced inset featuring the Pieced Heart design (pages 158 and 159). Narrow edging strips add definition to each side of the band. Stitch-in-the-ditch quilting is used on the Pieced Heart band. The upper and lower sections of the bunting can be quilted, using one of the other quilting techniques on pages 100 to 108, including channel quilting, stipple quilting, or motif quilting.

The lined bunting has a center front zipper opening for convenience. Boxed corners at the bottom give dimension to the bag, allowing room for the baby to move. The finished bunting is about 18" (46 cm) wide and 27" (68.5 cm) long, and can accommodate a blanket, if additional warmth is desired. A smaller bunting can be made by using five quilt blocks and trimming 2" (5 cm) from the length of the bunting.

✂ Cutting Directions

From the outer fabric, cut one 5½" (14 cm) strip for the upper section of the bunting and one 16½" (41.8 cm) strip for the lower section, cutting across the width of the fabric. The sections are cut to the correct widths on page 250.

For the border, cut two 1" (2.5 cm) strips each from two fabrics; the strips must be at least 39" (99 cm) long.

YOU WILL NEED

¾ yd. (0.7 m) outer fabric, for upper and lower sections of bunting.

Fabric scraps, for Pieced Heart blocks and border strips; or ¼ yd. (0.25 m) each of at least two fabrics for hearts and two fabrics for background.

1 yd. (0.95 m) backing fabric.

1 yd. (0.95 m) lining fabric.

Low-loft batting, about 34" × 42" (86.5 × 107 cm).

18" (46 cm) zipper.

How to Sew a Pieced Heart Baby Bunting

1) **Follow** steps 1 to 8 on page 159 to make two Pieced Heart quilt blocks. Repeat twice, using different fabrics, if desired, to make six blocks.

2) **Arrange** blocks into a horizontal row as desired; stitch blocks together along the sides in ¼" (6 mm) seams. Cut two 1¼" × 6½" (3.2 × 16.3 cm) strips for the extensions and facings at the ends of pieced band; cut strips from background fabrics that match the block fabrics at the ends of the band.

3) **Stitch** strips for extensions and facings to ends of band in ¼" (6 mm) seams. Press seam allowances toward the facing. Extension and facing strips extend the band to allow for a ¾" (2 cm) seam allowance at center front of the bunting. Measure width of band, including extensions and facings.

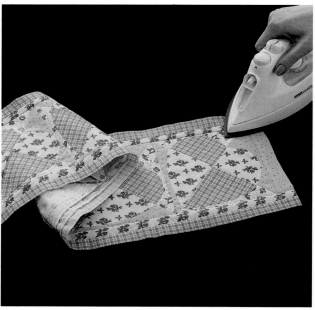

4) **Trim** upper and lower sections of bunting and border strips to measurement determined in step 3. Stitch two border strips together lengthwise, right sides together, in ¼" (6 mm) seam. Stitch pieced strip to upper edge of pieced band. Repeat at lower edge of band with the remaining two strips. Press the seam allowances away from Pieced Heart blocks.

5) Stitch pieced band to upper and lower bunting sections in ¼" (6 mm) seams. Press seam allowances toward band. Mark the quilting design lines on upper and lower sections of the bunting, if necessary, as on page 102.

6) Cut backing 4" (10 cm) wider and longer than quilt top. Layer and baste the quilt top, batting, and backing (pages 96 to 99). Quilt (pages 100 to 108); use stitch-in-the-ditch method on the pieced band and channel quilting, stipple quilting, or motif quilting on upper and lower sections.

7) Trim batting and backing fabric even with edges of quilt top. Measure length and width of quilt top; cut lining fabric to this size.

8) Pin-mark position of zipper bottom stop on center front seam allowance, with zipper tab at upper edge of pieced band. Pin quilt top, right sides together, at the center front. Machine-baste center front seam the length of the zipper, ¾" (2 cm) from edge; stitch the seam below zipper, using regular stitch length.

(Continued on next page)

9) Press the seam allowances to flatten batting. Press seam open, using tip of iron.

10) Apply glue stick lightly to the face side of zipper. Place zipper facedown on seam, aligning zipper coil to seamline; press down to secure. Hand-baste zipper tape to seam allowances through all layers.

11) Turn bunting right side out; pin-mark bottom stop of zipper. Using zipper foot, topstitch around zipper about ¼" (6 mm) from seamline; in the pieced section, stitch in the ditch of the seam along the facing strip. In the lower section, center ½" (1.3 cm) transparent tape over seamline to use as a guide.

12) Fold lining right sides together; pin in place, and mark zipper stop. Stitch ¾" (2 cm) center front seam, from the lower edge to 1" (2.5 cm) below zipper stop. Press seam open.

13) Pin lining to outer fabric, right sides together, at upper edge and front edges. Stitch a ¼" (6 mm) seam allowance at upper edge and ¾" (2 cm) seam allowance at front edges; start and end stitching about 1" (2.5 cm) above zipper.

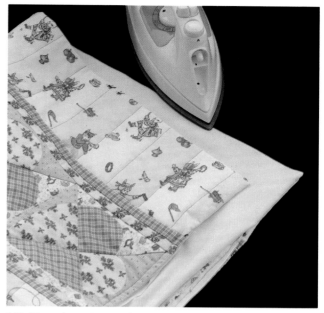

14) Trim corners diagonally; trim and taper seam allowances at front edges.

15) Turn bunting right side out. Lightly press upper and front edges.

16) Turn the bunting wrong side out. Smooth the lining into position, matching center front seams; pin along lower edge. Fold under seam allowances of lining at center front; pin. Slipstitch lining to zipper tape.

17) Stitch a ¼" (6 mm) seam at the lower edge; finish seam, using a zigzag or overlock stitch. Stitch about 4½" (11.5 cm) across the corners through all the layers as shown, to make boxed corners. Turn bunting right side out.

18) Topstitch upper edge and front edges, overlapping stitches at upper edge of zipper.

Alternate Piecing Techniques

String-pieced Quilts

String piecing is an easy way to create interesting and lively fabric arrangements. Traditionally used to make utility quilts, string piecing also lends itself to many contemporary designs.

String piecing is done on a foundation of fabric or paper. Strips of fabric in various widths are stitched to the foundation, and the completed blocks can be arranged for a variety of effects.

Lightweight muslin works well for the foundation. When string-piecing heavyweight fabrics, such as decorator fabrics, use a paper foundation to reduce bulk; the paper is removed from the completed block. Unprinted newsprint, available in large tablets, may be used as a foundation and is easy to remove.

Basic instructions are given on page 258 for making string-pieced quilt blocks of any size or shape. This technique is used for making all styles of string-pieced quilts, including those shown on page 261.

The color-graduated quilt shown opposite is a quick project make by string piecing. The gradation is easily achieved by the arrangement of light, medium, and dark quilt blocks. Hand-dyed fabrics work especially well for this project.

The instructions on pages 259 and 260 are for a color-graduated quilt made from thirty-two 8" (20.5 cm) quilt blocks. The finished quilt measures about 40" × 71" (102 × 180.5 cm), making it suitable for a wall hanging or lap quilt.

✂ Cutting Directions

For the color-graduated quilt, cut muslin foundation fabric into thirty-two 9" (23 cm) squares; this is the finished block size plus 1" (2.5 cm). Cut fabrics of light, medium, and dark colors into strips about 3" to 4" (7.5 to 10 cm) wide.

YOU WILL NEED

1¾ yd. (1.6 m) **lightweight muslin** for foundation fabric.

¼ yd. (0.25 m) **fabric** in each of five light, five medium, and five dark colors that blend, for a color-graduated quilt.

⅞ yd. (0.8 m) **fabric** for 4" (10 cm) border.

2¼ yd. (2.1 m) **fabric** for backing.

⅔ yd. (0.63 m) **fabric** for binding.

Batting, about 44" x 75" (112 × 190.5 cm).

Strips of fabric are stitched onto a square or rectangle of foundation fabric or paper, and the edges are trimmed to make a string-pieced quilt block. The strips may be placed horizontally, vertically, or diagonally.

How to Make a String-pieced Quilt Block

1) Cut a muslin or paper foundation 1" (2.5 cm) larger than finished block size. Cut strips of fabric, varying the width as desired; the cut length should extend beyond the edges of the foundation.

2) Place one strip, right side up, in the middle area of the foundation at desired angle; ends of strip should extend beyond edges of foundation. Pin in place.

3) Place second strip, right side down, along one long edge of first strip; pin. Stitch ¼" (6 mm) from aligned raw edges.

4) Fold strip right side up; press. Continue adding strips until half of foundation is covered. If desired, change angle of some strips, and stitch ¼" (6 mm) from raw edge of top strip; trim edges of strips even.

5) Repeat steps 3 and 4 for the opposite side of the foundation.

6) Trim block to finished size plus ½" (1.3 cm) for seam allowances. Remove paper foundation, if used.

How to Make a String-pieced Quilt with Color Gradations

1) Separate the fabric strips into light, medium, and dark colors. Make eight string-pieced blocks (opposite), using light colors and setting strips on the diagonal; trim blocks to 8½" (21.8 cm) squares. These will be first and second rows of quilt.

2) Make four blocks, using some light and some medium fabrics in each block, for third row.

3) Make eight blocks, using medium colors; these will be fourth and fifth rows. Make four blocks, using some medium and some dark fabrics, for sixth row.

4) Make eight blocks, using dark colors; these will be seventh and eighth rows. Arrange blocks in all rows so strips form a zigzag pattern, as shown.

(Continued on next page)

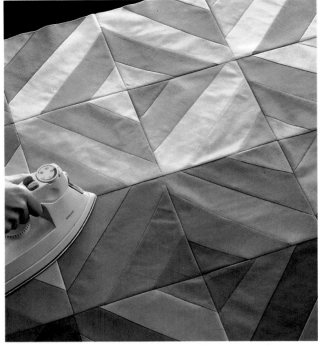

5) Stitch each row of four blocks together. Stitch rows together, finger-pressing seams in opposite directions. Press quilt top.

6) Cut and attach border strips (pages 84 to 89); the cut width of border strips is 4½" (11.5 cm). Using a straightedge, mark borders for quilting by randomly extending lines into the border.

7) Cut backing about 4" (10 cm) larger than quilt top; press. Layer and baste quilt top, batting, and backing (pages 96 to 99). Quilt on all seamlines, using stitch-in-the-ditch method (pages 104 and 105); extend stitching into border on marked lines.

8) Cut and apply binding (pages 112 and 113); cut width of binding is 2½" (6.5 cm). For wall hanging, attach fabric sleeve (page 165).

More String-pieced Designs

Vary the width and angle of the fabric strips for different effects. For a contemporary look, use bold colors or mix in specialty fabrics for drama. Experiment with different fabrics, block sizes, and block arrangements.

Decorator fabrics, cut in wide strips, make a quick and easy bed quilt. The full-size coverlet shown below consists of thirty-six 12" (30.5 cm) quilt blocks, six across and six down. The finished size of the quilt, including a 4" (10 cm) border, is about 80" (203.5 cm) square.

Contemporary look is achieved in this quilt by string-piecing long foundation strips instead of blocks.

Lap Quilts

This generously sized lap quilt uses a patterned striped fabric and easy strip piecing to make a quilt top that looks intricate. Six pieced strips are separated with sashing, cut from the striped fabric; and a mitered border, also cut from the striped fabric, frames the quilt.

For the sashing and border, choose a patterned striped fabric that can be cut lengthwise into strips. Most quilt shops carry suitable designs. The fabrics may include florals, paisleys, and other motifs. In order to cut the sashing and border strips from one length of fabric, you will need a striped fabric from which you can cut five sashing strips and four border strips.

The six pieced fabric strips that alternate with the sashing strips are made from six coordinating fabrics. When selecting the fabric colors, look for light, medium, and dark fabrics.

The finished size of the lap quilt varies, depending on the width of the sashing and border. The quilt shown opposite measures 56" × 68" (142 × 173 cm); the sashing has a finished width of 3½" (9 cm) and the border has a finished width of 4¼" (10.8 cm).

Use ¼" (6 mm) seam allowances in the instructions that follow. Stitch accurately, so the pieces will fit exactly. If you have a seam guide on your sewing machine, check the placement of the ¼" (6 mm) mark by stitching on a scrap of fabric. If the machine does not have a ¼" (6 mm) seam guide, mark one on the bed of the machine with tape.

✂ Cutting Directions

Cut the patterned striped fabric lengthwise to make four border strips and five sashing strips; the cut width of the strips is equal to the desired finished width plus ½" (1.3 cm) for two ¼" (6 mm) seam allowances. The cut length of the sashing strips is 60½" (153.8 cm). The border strips will be trimmed to the correct length on page 265, step 6.

Cut each of the ½-yd. (0.5 m) fabric pieces into four 3" (7.5 cm) strips, cutting the strips on the crosswise grain.

Cut the binding fabric into 2½" (6.5 cm) strips, cutting the strips on the crosswise grain.

Patterned striped fabric is cut lengthwise to make four border strips and five sashing strips. Use the design of the fabric as a guide for determining the width of the strips, and add ¼" (6 mm) seam allowance on each side of the strips.

YOU WILL NEED

2¼ yd. (2.1 m) patterned striped fabric, for sashing and border.

Six fabrics, ½ yd. (0.5 m) each, for pieced strips, in prints to coordinate with patterned striped fabric.

⅝ yd. (0.6 m) fabric, for binding.

3½ yd. (3.2 m) fabric, for backing.

Low-loft quilt batting in twin size.

Safety pins, for basting quilt layers.

How to Sew a Lap Quilt

1) **Stitch** together, lengthwise, one 3" (7.5 cm) strip of each fabric for the pieced strips, with right sides together and in the desired sequence. Repeat three more times, stitching in the same sequence, to make four pieced units. Press all seam allowances in the same direction.

2) **Fold** one pieced fabric unit in half crosswise. Cut the pieced unit crosswise into 5½" (14 cm) strips to make six strips; discard excess fabric. Repeat for the remaining pieced units to make twenty-four strips.

3) **Stitch** four strips together, end to end, in same sequence, to make one strip of twenty-four pieces of fabric. Repeat five times to make a total of six pieced fabric strips.

4) **Place** one sashing strip and one pieced strip right sides together; match and pin centers and ends. Pin along the length, easing in any excess fullness; stitch.

5) **Stitch** another pieced strip to the other side of the sashing. Continue stitching strips together, alternating sashing and pieced strips, until six pieced strips and five sashing strips are stitched together. Press seam allowances toward sashing.

6) Measure quilt top across middle. Cut two border strips, with length equal to this measurement plus two times finished width of border plus 1" (2.5 cm); cut width is equal to finished width of border plus ½" (1.3 cm). Repeat for side strips, measuring down the middle from top to bottom.

7) Mark center of quilt top at upper and lower edges; mark center of upper and lower border strips. From each end of border strips, mark the finished width of the border plus ½" (1.3 cm). Place upper border strip on quilt top, right sides together, matching pin marks at center.

8) Match markings at ends of strip to edges of quilt top; pin. Pin along length, easing in any fullness. Stitch, beginning and ending ¼" (6 mm) from edges of quilt top; backstitch at ends. Repeat at lower edge.

9) Repeat steps 7 and 8 for the sides of the quilt top.

10) Fold the quilt top diagonally at corner, with right sides together and matching border seamlines; pin securely. Draw a diagonal line on the border strip, extending the line formed by fold of quilt top.

(Continued on next page)

11) Stitch on the marked line; do not catch the seam allowances in stitching. Trim ends of border strips to ¼" (6 mm) from stitching.

12) Press seam allowances open at corner; press the remaining seam allowances toward the border strip. Repeat for remaining corners.

13) Cut the backing fabric 4" to 8" (10 to 20.5 cm) larger than quilt top; piece fabric as necessary and trim off selvages before stitching. Place backing wrong side up on a flat surface; tape backing taut, from center of each side, toward corners.

14) Center batting on backing. Place quilt top, right side up, on batting. Smooth, but do not stretch. Baste layers together, using safety pins, working from center out, and placing pins about every 6" (15 cm). Remove tape from backing.

15) Quilt by stitching along border strips, then along seamlines of sashing strips and pieced sections. Apply binding (opposite).

How to Apply the Binding to the Lap Quilt

1) Stitch two binding strips together, stitching seam on the bias; trim the seam allowances to ¼" (6 mm). Repeat for the remaining strips to make four binding strips. Press binding strips in half lengthwise, wrong sides together.

2) Measure quilt top across middle. Cut two binding strips equal to this measurement plus 2" (5 cm). Mark binding strips 1" (2.5 cm) from ends; divide area between pins in fourths, and pin-mark. Divide upper and lower edges of quilt in fourths; pin-mark.

3) Pin binding strip to upper edge of quilt top, matching raw edges and pin marks; binding will extend 1" (2.5 cm) beyond ends of quilt top at each end. Stitch a scant ¼" (6 mm) from raw edges.

4) Trim excess batting and backing to a scant ½" (1.3 cm) from the stitching. Wrap binding strip snugly around edge of quilt, covering the stitching line on back of quilt; pin in the ditch of the seam.

5) Stitch in the ditch on the right side of quilt top by stitching over the seamline in the well of seam; catch binding on back of quilt in the stitching.

6) Repeat steps 3 to 5 for the lower edge of quilt. Trim ends of upper and lower binding strips even with edges of quilt top.

7) Repeat steps 2 and 3 for sides. Trim the ends of the binding strips to extend ½" (1.3 cm) beyond the finished edges of the quilt. Trim the excess batting and backing to scant ½" (1.3 cm) from stitching.

8) Fold the ½" (1.3 cm) end of the binding over finished edge. Wrap binding to back of quilt and stitch as in steps 4 and 5. Slipstitch ends.

Appliquéd Quilts

Three different methods of machine appliqué are popular for appliquéd quilts: blindstitched, frayed, and satin-stitched. Each method has a different look and can be used to match the style of the quilt, from traditional to contemporary.

Blindstitched appliqué has the look of traditional hand stitching, but uses a faster machine technique. The appliqué is stitched to the quilt block using monofilament nylon thread for the needle thread and the machine blindstitch. The appliqués are made by shaping the fabric around cardboard templates. The templates do not include seam allowances; estimated ¼" (6 mm) seam allowances are added when the fabric is cut. Bias tape may be used for flower stems or wherever a narrow strip is needed, eliminating the need for a template.

Frayed appliqué has exposed raw edges. To secure the appliqué, the stitching is done inside the edges of the design. For a frayed appearance, the appliqué is then brushed with a stiff brush, or, provided the fabrics have been prewashed, a more natural frayed look can be achieved by laundering. Frayed appliqué

gives added texture and interest to a quilt and has a more contemporary look.

Satin-stitched appliqué has machine satin stitching that secures the appliqué and covers the raw edges of the fabric, for a more defined appearance. Use this method for easier application of intricately shaped pieces or appliqués cut from printed fabric. Satin-stitch appliqué is durable and is therefore a good choice for quilts that will be laundered frequently.

When stitching appliqués, decrease the needle thread tension and use a bobbin thread that matches the quilt top. To prevent the appliqués from puckering, apply a piece of tear-away stabilizer to the wrong side of the quilt top.

The instructions that follow are for the Garden Row Appliqué Sampler, above. This project incorporates all three methods of appliqué and may be used as a table runner or wall hanging. The sampler is made from five quilt blocks, each measuring 6½" × 8½" (16.3 × 21.8 cm). The finished project measures about 35½" × 11½" (90.3 × 29.3 cm).

Types of Appliqués

Blindstitched appliqué resembles traditional hand stitching but is sewn with the machine blindstitch.

Frayed appliqué is a contemporary style with exposed raw edges.

Satin-stitched appliqué, sewn with machine satin stitching, has more defined edges.

✂ Cutting Directions

Cut five 7" × 9" (18 × 23 cm) rectangles from fabric background.

For tulips on two quilt blocks, use the patterns on page 270 to make cardboard templates for the tulip flower and tulip leaf. Cut six flowers and six leaves from fabric as on page 272; step 1; turn the template over to cut two of the leaves. Cut six stems from bias tape to desired lengths. Three leaves, three flowers, and three stems are used for each quilt block.

For geraniums on two quilt blocks, cut six leaves and 16 to 20 florets, using the patterns on page 270. Cut two fabric stems ¼" × 3" (6 × 7.5 cm). Three leaves, eight to ten florets, and one stem are used for each quilt block.

For hibiscus on one quilt block, cut two flowers and two leaves, using the patterns on page 270; turn the pattern over to cut one of the leaves.

YOU WILL NEED

⅜ yd. (0.35 m) fabric for background.

¾ yd. (0.7 m) fabric for 1½" (3.8 cm) border, backing, and binding.

Fabric scraps for flowers and leaves; double-fold bias tape for tulip stems.

Batting, about 13" × 35" (33 × 89 cm).

Cardboard, spray starch, and monofilament nylon thread for blindstitched appliqués.

¾ yd. (0.7 m) tear-away stabilizer.

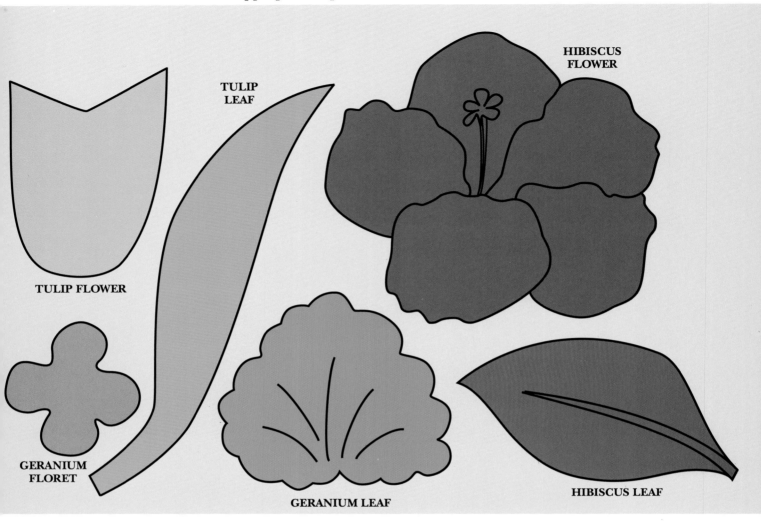

TULIP
LEAF

HIBISCUS
FLOWER

TULIP FLOWER

GERANIUM
FLORET

GERANIUM LEAF

HIBISCUS LEAF

How to Make a Garden Row Appliqué Sampler

1) Follow steps 2 to 5 on page 272 for the blindstitched appliqués, arranging pieces for three tulips on quilt block as shown; place bottom of leaves at raw edge of block. For stems, trim away one folded edge of bias tape to reduce bulk. Repeat for second quilt block.

2) Follow steps 1 to 7 on page 273 for the frayed appliqués, arranging pieces for one geranium on quilt block as shown. Repeat for second quilt block.

3) Follow steps 1 to 4 on page 274 for the satin-stitched appliqués, arranging pieces for two hibiscus flowers on quilt block as shown.

4) Stitch stamens on hibiscus, using free-motion sewing (page 100).

5) Stitch blocks together in ¼" (6 mm) seams, as shown. Press the quilt top, taking care not to overpress appliqués.

6) Cut and attach border strips (pages 84 to 89); cut width of border strips is 2" (5 cm). Cut backing 13" × 35" (33 × 89 cm); layer and baste the quilt top, batting, and backing (pages 96 to 99).

7) Quilt, using stitch-in-the-ditch method, along the seamlines (pages 104 and 105). Quilt around flowers. If desired, quilt along design lines of hibiscus, to define petals. (Contrasting thread was used to show detail.)

8) Cut and apply binding (pages 112 and 113); cut width of binding is 2" (5 cm). For wall hanging, attach fabric sleeve (page 165).

How to Sew a Blindstitched Appliqué

1) Cut cardboard templates to the *finished size* of appliqué pieces. Place template on fabric. Adding 1/4" (6 mm) seam allowances, cut around template, using rotary cutter. Clip inside curves and corners almost to template; trim outside corners.

2) Spray starch in small bowl; dab starch on section of seam allowance. With tip of dry iron, press seam allowance over edge of template; press until spray starch dries. Continue pressing around the appliqué. Remove the template, and press appliqué, right side up.

3) Position appliqué design on the quilt block; mark the placement of the pieces, using chalk. Position tear-away stabilizer, cut larger than design, on wrong side of fabric. Pin or baste pieces in place; for layered design, apply first layer only.

4) Set machine for short blindstitch, with the stitch width about 1/16" (1.5 mm); use monofilament nylon thread in the needle. Blindstitch around pieces, catching edge with widest swing of stitch. (Contrasting thread was used to show detail.)

5) Pin or baste the second layer in place, and blindstitch. Repeat as necessary for any remaining layers. Remove tear-away stabilizer, taking care not to distort stitches.

How to Sew a Frayed Appliqué

1) Cut the appliqué pieces, using patterns; do not add seam allowances. Mark any design lines.

2) Position the appliqué design on quilt block; mark the placement of pieces, using chalk.

3) Glue-baste pieces in place ¼" (6 mm) from edges; for layered design, apply first layer only. Place tear-away stabilizer on wrong side of fabric.

4) Stitch around pieces, stitching ⅛" (3 mm) from raw edge; some designs may require free-motion stitching (page 100).

5) Glue-baste the second layer in place; stitch as in step 4. Repeat as necessary for any remaining layers.

6) Stitch on any design lines, using free-motion sewing, if necessary. Remove tear-away stabilizer, taking care not to distort stitches.

7) Brush edges of appliqué, if desired, using a stiff brush; this will ravel edges to add more texture.

How to Sew a Satin-stitched Appliqué

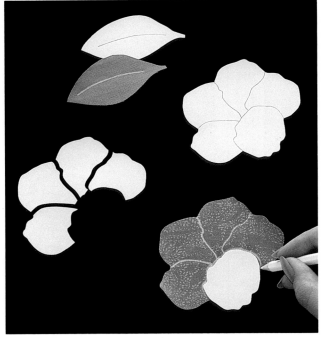

1) **Cut** appliqué pieces, using patterns; do not add seam allowances. Mark any design lines; patterns may be cut apart to serve as guide for marking.

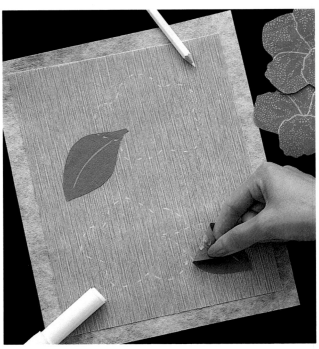

2) **Position** pieces on quilt block; mark placement, using chalk. Position tear-away stabilizer on wrong side of fabric. Glue-baste or pin pieces in place; for layered design, apply first layer only.

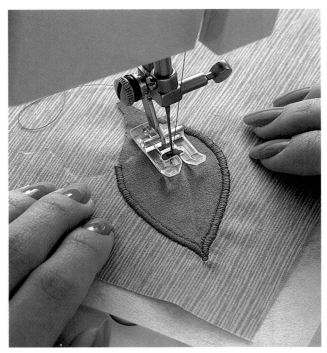

3) **Set** machine for short, wide zigzag stitch; use machine embroidery thread in needle. Satin stitch around pieces; do not satin stitch edges that will be overlapped by other pieces. Add details, such as veins of leaves; for veins, use narrow zigzag stitch and taper ends.

4) **Glue-baste** second layer in place; satin stitch as in step 3. Repeat for any remaining layers. Remove the tear-away stabilizer, taking care not to distort stitches.

Satin-stitching Techniques for Appliqués

Curves. Pivot the fabric frequently, pivoting with the needle down. For inside curves, pivot with needle at inner edge of stitching (**a**); for outside curves, pivot with needle on outer edge of stitching (**b**).

Inside corners. Stitch past corner a distance equal to width of stitch, stopping with the needle down at the inner edge of stitching. Pivot fabric, and satin stitch next side of appliqué.

Outside corners. Stitch one stitch past edge of appliqué, stopping with needle down at outer edge of stitching. Pivot fabric, and satin stitch next side of appliqué.

Points. 1) Stitch, stopping when inner edge of satin stitching meets the opposite side of the appliqué. Pivot the fabric slightly; continue stitching, gradually narrowing stitch width to 0 and stopping at point. (Presser foot was removed to show detail.)

2) Pivot fabric, and stitch back over previous stitches, gradually widening the stitch width to original width. Pivot fabric slightly, and stitch next side of appliqué.

More Appliqué Designs

The appliqué methods used for the Garden Row Appliqué Sampler can be used for many designs. Use the appliqué patterns available at quilt stores, or design your own appliqués, using books, cards, and artwork for design ideas.

Frayed appliqué and authentic African prints were used for the quilt above. Primitive figures were made from two fabric layers, the top layer cut smaller than the first.

Blindstitched appliqué is used for the quilt at left. The easy-to-cut pieces are blindstitched in place.

Satin-stitched appliqué (opposite) is used for the fish, which were cut from a printed fabric. A string-pieced quilt top (page 257) provides the background; some strips were pieced together before they were applied to the foundation.

Lone Star Wall Hanging with Flower Appliqués

Brighten a wall with this dramatic wall hanging that combines the Lone Star design with dimensional appliqués. The Lone Star design is made from eight hand-dyed fabrics that graduate from light to dark, from the center of the star out to the points. A contrasting fabric is also used to create a circle of interest within the star. The center of the quilt is embellished with dimensional leaves and yo-yo flowers, attached to a vine made from double-fold bias tape. Select fabrics for the leaves and yo-yo flowers that repeat the colors found in the background fabric. The finished wall hanging measures about 43½" (110.5 cm) square.

✂ Cutting Directions

Cut strips from hand-dyed fabrics and insert fabric for the Lone Star design as in steps 1 and 2.

Cut four 11" (28 cm) squares from background fabric. Also cut one 16⅛" (40.8 cm) square from background fabric. Cut the square diagonally through opposite corners in both directions to make four triangles.

Cut four 1½" (3.8 cm) strips from Fabric H, for the inner border. Cut five 3½" (9 cm) strips from the fabric for the outer border. Cut five 2" (5 cm) strips from the fabric for the binding.

Cut ten leaves, using the leaf pattern (page 285), with fabric right sides together as on page 284, step 21. Cut ten circles, using patterns for yo-yo flowers as on page 285, step 24.

YOU WILL NEED

½-yd. (0.5 m) bundle of eight hand-dyed fabrics in a light to dark gradation; or ¼ yd. (0.25 m) each of eight fabrics for Lone Star design and inner border.

⅓ yd. (0.32 m) black or other dark fabric that contrasts with hand-dyed fabrics, for insert fabric.

1 yd. (0.95 m) fabric, for background and binding.

⅝ yd. (0.6 m) fabric, for outer border.

1½ yd. (1.4 m) fabric, for backing.

Batting, about 52" (132 cm) square.

¼ yd. (0.25 m) fabric, for flower appliqués.

¼ yd. (0.25 m) fabric, for leaf appliqués.

1 package narrow double-fold bias tape, for vine.

6" × 24" (15 × 61 cm) plexiglass ruler, for cutting at 45° angle.

Tear-away stabilizer.

How to Sew a Lone Star Wall Hanging with Flower Appliqués

1) Label eight hand-dyed fabrics from A to H, with A being the lightest fabric and H being the darkest. Place Fabric A and Fabric H together, matching raw edges; fold in half. Cut 2" (5 cm) strip across fabrics. Repeat with Fabrics B and G, cutting two strips from each fabric.

2) Cut three 2" (5 cm) strips from Fabrics C and F. Cut four 2" (5 cm) strips from Fabrics D and E. Cut five 2" (5 cm) strips from insert fabric. Arrange the fabric strips in order from A to H, placing the insert fabric between Fabrics D and E.

(Continued on next page)

3) Stitch one strip of Fabric A to one strip of Fabric B, right sides together, along one long edge. Stitch one strip of Fabric C to long edge of Fabric B of pieced unit. Continue to stitch strips from Fabric D and insert fabric to unit in order to make a strip set. Press seam allowances toward lightest fabrics.

4) Stitch strips of Fabrics B, C, D, insert, and E together as in step 3 to make a strip set. Press seam allowances toward darkest fabrics. Stitch strips of Fabrics C, D, insert, E, and F together to make third strip set; press seam allowances toward lightest fabrics. Stitch strips of Fabrics D, insert, E, F, and G together to make fourth strip set; press seam allowances toward darkest fabrics. Stitch strips of insert fabric, Fabrics E, F, G, and H together; press seam allowances toward lightest fabrics.

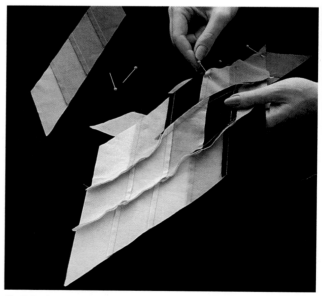

5) Cut ends of strip sets at 45° angles, using plexiglass ruler, keeping strips in order stitched in steps 3 and 4. Cut eight 2" (5 cm) diagonal strips from each strip set as shown. After every few strips, check 45° angle and recut edge, if necessary. Take care not to stretch bias edges. Stack strips together and arrange in order as shown.

6) Stitch strip from each stack together in order shown in step 5, pinning strips together at seam intersections; do not press seam allowances open. Repeat to make a total of eight pieced diamonds.

7) Mark wrong side of diamonds where ¼" (6 mm) seams will intersect, placing dots at the wide-angle corners. Mark the wrong sides of background pieces where ¼" (6 mm) seams will intersect, placing dots at right-angle corner of triangles and at one corner of each square.

8) Stitch two diamonds, right sides together, along one side, from the inner point of Fabric A to dot, pinning the strips together at seam intersections and finger-pressing seam allowances in opposite directions; backstitch at dot. Repeat for remaining diamonds.

9) Stitch two 2-diamond units right sides together, as in step 8, finger-pressing seam allowances in opposite directions. Repeat with remaining units to make two 4-diamond units. Stitch units together along the long edge, between the dots, pinning at seam intersections; backstitch at dots. Press star carefully, taking care not to stretch fabric.

10) Align short side of triangle to a diamond, right sides together, matching edges at outer point **(a)** and dots at inner point **(b)**. Stitch from the outer edge exactly to dot, with diamond side up; backstitch.

(Continued on next page)

11) Align remaining side of triangle to adjoining diamond, and stitch as in step 10, with triangle side up. Repeat for the remaining triangles, stitching them between every other set of points on the star.

12) Align squares to the sides of diamonds between remaining points of star, matching edges at outer point **(a)** and dots at inner point **(b);** stitch with diamond side up, as in step 10. Align remaining sides of squares and diamonds; stitch with square side up.

13) Release stitching within seam allowances at center of star, so seam allowances will lie flat. Press from wrong side, working from center out. Cut and apply inner border as on page 86, steps 1 to 3.

14) Measure horizontally through middle of quilt top and cut two outer border strips to that length for the upper and lower outer borders; stitch to quilt top as for inner border. Piece remaining outer border strips together (page 84). Measure vertically through middle of quilt top, including outer border strips, and cut two outer border strips for sides equal to this length; stitch to quilt as for inner border.

15) Cut 40" (102 cm) length of bias tape; trim off one fold of tape on narrower side to reduce bulk. Pin tape to center of star, making a wavy circle as shown; butt the ends together. Position tear-away stabilizer, cut larger than design, on wrong side of the fabric.

16) Set machine for short blindstitch, with the stitch width about ⅛" (3 mm); use monofilament nylon thread in the needle. (Contrasting thread was used to show detail.) Blindstitch around bias tape, catching the edge with widest swing of the stitch; remove tear-away stabilizer.

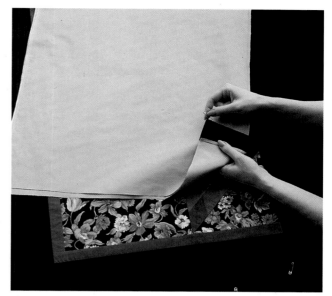

17) Cut backing fabric 2" to 4" (5 to 10 cm) wider and longer than quilt top, piecing with outer border fabric, if desired. Mark center of each side of quilt top and backing fabric with safety pins.

18) Mark quilting design lines on the background squares and borders by extending seamlines of star out to edges of quilt top. Mark quilting lines on the background triangles 1½" (3.8 cm) from the sides of triangle, extending lines into borders. Continue to mark additional lines on triangles 1½" (3.8 cm) from previous markings as shown.

19) Layer and baste the quilt as on pages 96 to 99. Stitch in the ditch (pages 104 and 105) in the seam-lines of the star, from the bias tape out; extend stitching into the borders, following marked lines. Quilt background triangles by stitching on marked lines; begin and end stitching at the raw edge of the border.

(Continued on next page)

20) Stipple-quilt (page 106) the center of quilt inside circle of bias tape. Attach fabric sleeve as on page 165. Apply binding as on pages 112 and 113.

21) Trace pattern for leaf (opposite) onto tracing paper. Fold fabric for leaves right sides together; cut ten sets of leaves, using leaf pattern. Trim some leaves narrower or shorter to vary the shapes slightly.

22) Stitch leaves, right sides together, ⅛" (3 mm) from raw edges, crossing over the beginning of stitching at end. Cut a slit in one layer, and turn leaf right side out, using a point tool to smooth outer edges from inside. Repeat for remaining leaves. Press leaves. Transfer markings for veins onto leaves.

23) Pin leaves to bias tape vine, covering the ends of bias tape with one leaf. Stitch leaves to quilt along the vein lines, using free-motion stitching (page 100).

24) Trace partial pattern for each size of circle onto tracing paper, placing dotted line on fold of paper. Cut on solid lines; open full-size circle patterns for yo-yo flowers. From each yo-yo pattern, cut five circles from fabric for flowers.

25) Turn ¼" (6 mm) of circle to wrong side, and stitch hand running stitches a scant ⅛" (3 mm) from folded edge. Pull up thread to gather circle, and tie off threads on the inside. Repeat with remaining circles. Pin yo-yo flowers to vine; position button in center, and hand-stitch in place.

Yo-Yo Flowers and Leaf Appliqués

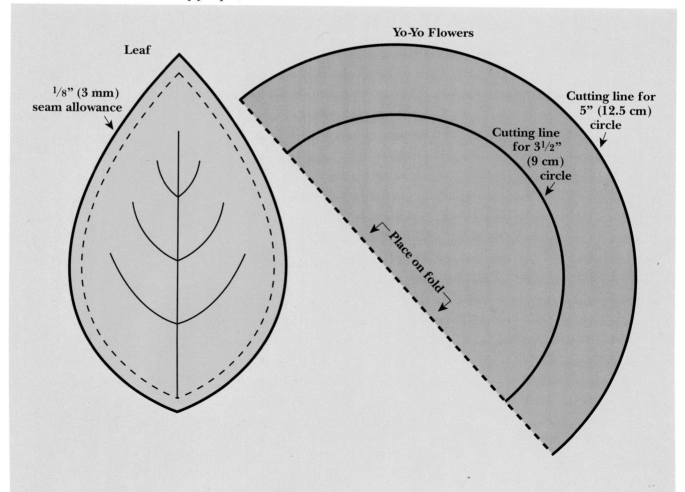

Leaf

⅛" (3 mm) seam allowance

Yo-Yo Flowers

Cutting line for 5" (12.5 cm) circle

Cutting line for 3½" (9 cm) circle

Place on fold

Tumbling Hexagon Wall Hanging

British patchworkers have long used paper piecing for all their designs. Today, it is used for quilt patterns that do not lend themselves well to machine sewing, such as those with no long rows to sew and pieces that need to fit together exactly. Paper piecing is used in combination with machine stitching to produce an accurate, extremely flat quilt top in the least amount of time.

For the Tumbling Hexagon wall hanging, fabric hexagons are first hand-basted to paper cutouts. The hexagons are arranged in any pattern or color combination, then are machine-stitched together, one by one, using a zigzag stitch, which is visible from the front of the pieced unit. The hexagons are steamed before removing the paper pieces in order to keep the hexagons flat and straight.

The hexagons in this wall hanging are arranged in nine rows. Some hexagons are blindstitched to the quilt top as if they are falling away from the rows. Additional hexagons are double-faced and hung loosely on the quilt for a three-dimensional embellishment. The finished wall hanging measures about 26½" × 28¼" (67.3 × 71.7 cm).

✂ Cutting Directions

Make ten photocopies of the hexagon pattern on page 291. Cut the individual hexagons apart.

Cut the desired number of hexagons from each hexagon fabric for a total of 84 hexagons; cut the hexagons ¼" (6 mm) larger than the paper on all sides.

Cut one 27" × 29" (68.5 × 73.5 cm) rectangle from the border fabric.

Cut four 2" (5 cm) strips from the binding fabric.

YOU WILL NEED

⅛ yd. (0.15 m) each of ten or more different fabrics, for hexagons.

1 yd. (0.95 m) fabric, for border and binding.

⅞ yd. (0.8 m) fabric, for backing.

Batting, about 31" × 33" (78.5 × 84 cm).

Monofilament nylon thread.

Tear-away stabilizer.

Decorative thread.

Mediumweight fusible interfacing.

How to Sew a Tumbling Hexagon Wall Hanging

1) Pin paper hexagon to the back of fabric hexagon. Finger-press seam allowances to back of paper; hand-baste the hexagon to paper along seam allowances. Repeat for 75 additional hexagons.

2) Trace paper hexagon onto interfacing eight times; cut out hexagons. Follow step 1 to make eight more hexagons, substituting interfacing hexagons for the paper and fusing interfacing hexagons to the fabric, following manufacturer's instructions. Set aside these eight hexagons until step 11.

3) Arrange 76 hexagons on work surface in nine columns, alternating eight and nine hexagons in each column, in desired color sequence. Allow a few hexagons in last row to fall away from organized rows, as shown.

4) Stitch first two hexagons of first column, right sides together, using a zigzag stitch with a 1/16" (1.5 mm) stitch length and 1/16" (1.5 mm) stitch width, barely catching the fabric; backstitch at each end. If seam does not lie flat, loosen top thread tension. Repeat to stitch remaining hexagons together in column one. Repeat for remaining columns; set aside individual hexagons for tumbling from last row.

5) **Stitch** first two columns of hexagons together, one hexagon at a time, as on page 288, step 4. Continue to add columns until pieced unit is complete.

6) **Steam** pieced unit with paper hexagons still intact. Remove the basting stitches; steam a second time to remove basting marks. Remove the paper hexagons. Repeat with the individual hexagons reserved for tumbling from last row.

7) **Pin** or baste pieced unit to front of rectangle for border fabric. Position tear-away stabilizer, cut to size of border fabric, on wrong side of border fabric.

8) **Set** machine for short blindstitch, with the stitch width about 1/16" (1.5 mm); use monofilament nylon thread in the needle. Blindstitch around pieced unit, catching edge with widest swing of stitch. Remove tear-away stabilizer, taking care not to distort stitches.

(Continued on next page)

9) Cut backing fabric 2" to 4" (5 to 10 cm) wider and longer than quilt top. Layer and baste the quilt top, batting, and backing as on pages 96 to 99.

10) Quilt in long, flowing lines across quilt top in two directions, using walking foot. Attach fabric sleeve to wall hanging (page 165), and apply the binding as on pages 112 and 113.

11) Steam the eight interfacing hexagons. Remove the basting stitches; steam a second time to remove basting marks. Pin two hexagons right sides together; zigzag around five sides as on page 288, step 4. Turn right side out; press. Whipstitch along remaining side. Repeat with remaining hexagons.

12) Hand-stitch individual hexagons to border to appear to be falling away from pieced unit; hand-stitch faced hexagons to pieced unit and to lower edge of quilt.

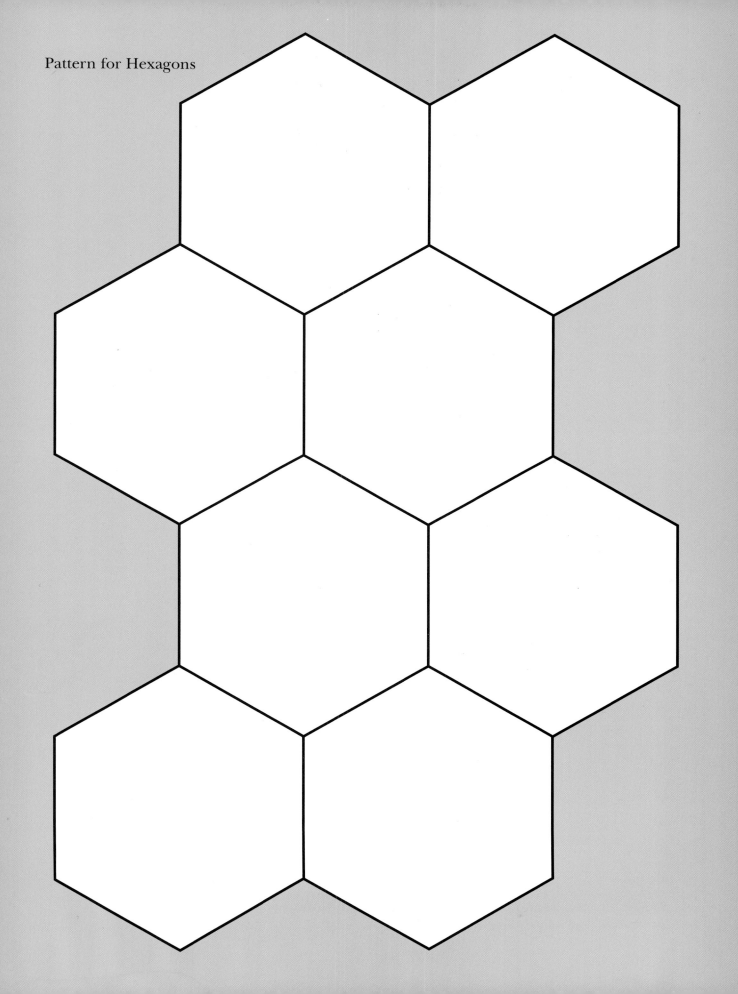

Pattern for Hexagons

Landscape Quilts

Strips of fabric can be used to portray landscapes, which are designed over a piece of foundation fabric. The strips are cut freehand, and the scene is created in layers, usually working from the top to the bottom. The exposed edges of the strips are turned under and secured with blindstitching. When designing landscapes, stand back and look at the project as you add the layered strips.

You may want to select fabrics that simulate the various textures of landscapes. Mottled prints, silk noils, and velveteens can be used to add depth to simple designs. For a country style, look for small calico prints to suggest texture.

Design inspiration can come from many sources. Photographs or paintings of landscapes can be adapted for landscape quilts. Before starting the project, you may want to make a sketch or actual-size drawing of the quilt.

YOU WILL NEED

> **Muslin** for foundation fabric.
> **Scraps of fabric** in choice of landscape colors.
> **Fabric for border,** yardage determined as on page 84.
> **Fabric for backing,** yardage determined as on page 31.
> **Fabric for binding,** yardage determined as on page 112.
> **Batting,** about 4" (10 cm) larger than quilt top.

Photographs are a good source of inspiration for landscape designs.

How to Make a Landscape Quilt

1) **Cut** foundation fabric slightly larger than finished landscape. Cut a fabric strip for the sky to the width of the foundation; pin to top of foundation.

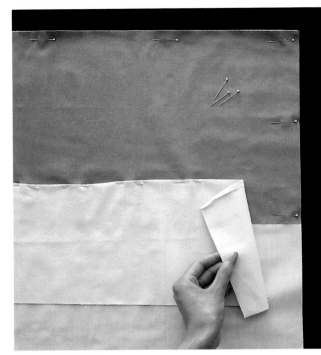

2) **Cut** the fabric strip for the next layer, the width of foundation, curving upper edge as desired. Pin strip to the foundation, covering lower edge of sky and folding under scant ¼" (6 mm) along upper edge; clip curves as necessary.

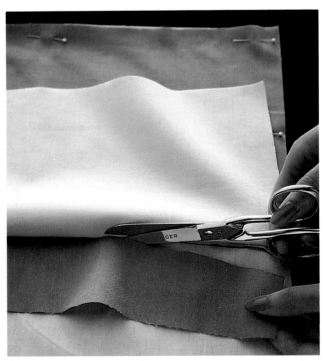

3) **View** pieces from a distance, with project on wall; adjust placement as desired. Trim excess fabric from previous layer.

4) **Continue** adding strips as in steps 2 and 3, until entire foundation is covered; some strips may be cut shorter to create hills or other landscaping details.

5) Cut additional shapes, such as clouds, and tuck behind a previous layer, if desired. Fold under exposed edges, or follow steps 1 and 2 on page 272 for blindstiched appliqué.

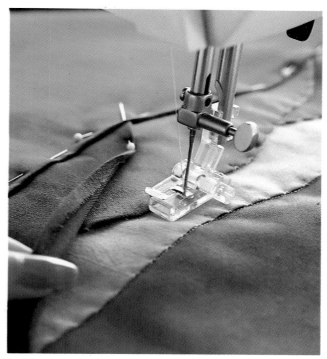

6) Blindstitch along pressed edges of strips, using monofilament nylon thread, as on page 272, step 4, folding back other layers as necessary. (Contrasting thread was used to show detail.)

7) Trim stitched landscape to finished size. Cut and attach border strips (pages 84 to 89). Cut backing and batting 4" (10 cm) larger than quilt top. Layer quilt top, batting, and backing (pages 96 to 99).

8) Quilt (pages 100 to 108); use stitch-in-the-ditch method along landscape strips and free-motion quilting for details. Cut and apply binding (pages 112 and 113). For wall hanging, attach fabric sleeve (page 165).

More Landscape Designs

To add details to a landscape quilt, incorporate appliqués into the quilt design. Quilting lines also add detailing.

Pueblo (left) is made of Tumbling Blocks (page 149), applied as on page 155. The doors, windows, and ladders are satin-stitched as on pages 274 and 275.

Sunrise (below) was applied starting with the yellow center and working toward the sides. The green section was applied next, then the colorful fields. The pine trees are appliquéd, using the frayed method (page 273).

Folk-art quilt (right) is created using textured fabrics. The farm structures, appliquéd using the blindstitched method (page 272), are intentionally "crooked" for a rustic, country look.

Sunset (below, right) is the starting point of this quilt. Then the cliffs and stream are applied, using the same landscaping method. The quilting lines create the sun's rays, add a rugged quality to the cliffs, and suggest movement of the water.

Crazy Quilts

Crazy quilting allows you to use scraps of all kinds to make quilts in an unplanned, nonprecise pattern. Crazy quilting was popular during the Victorian era, when scraps of silk were used to complement the lavish decorating style. Patches were basted on a foundation fabric and secured with hand embroidery stitches.

Today, machine embroidery makes these quilts faster to sew. Experiment with decorative threads, such as metallics and rayons, for embroidery stitches. Mix a variety of fabrics, such as satins, lamés, denims, and bits of old table or bed linens.

Crazy quilts can be sewn using either the traditional method or the stitch-and-flip method. For the traditional method, the patches are basted to a foundation fabric with the edges turned under, then secured with decorative stitches, such as feather and herringbone stitches. Or for faster construction, the patches can be arranged with the raw edges exposed; decorative satin stitches secure the patches and finish the edges. For the stitch-and-flip method, the patches are secured without decorative stitching. This method works well for quilts with a contemporary look.

Use a lightweight fabric, such as muslin, for the foundation, in a light color that will not show through the fabrics in the quilt top. The foundation fabric is usually cut into blocks, and the completed blocks sewn together to make the quilt top. For small quilts, the patches can be applied to one large foundation.

Traditionally, batting was not used with crazy quilts. To secure the quilt top to the backing, the quilts were tacked at the seamlines. If batting is used, the blocks should be tacked or quilted at frequent intervals to keep the batting from shifting.

Irregular patches of fabric are randomly stitched onto a square of foundation fabric, and the edges are trimmed to make a crazy-quilt block.

Tips for Making a Crazy Quilt

Use machine embroidery thread for smooth, even decorative stitching with sheen.

Control slippery fabrics, such as some silks, by fusing them to lightweight interfacing.

Use woven lamé for a decorative effect. Preshrink the lamé with a steam iron, and fuse it to knitted interfacing for strength and to prevent raveling.

Use a larger needle and loosen the needle thread tension when stitching with metallic thread. Check to see that the needle does not have burrs.

YOU WILL NEED

Fabric scraps for quilt blocks.

Lightweight muslin for foundation fabric.

Fabric for borders, if desired, yardage determined as on page 84.

Fabric for backing, yardage determined as on page 31.

Fabric for binding, yardage determined as on page 112.

Batting, if desired, about 4" (10 cm) larger than quilt.

Machine embroidery thread for a crazy quilt made by traditional method.

How to Make a Crazy Quilt Using the Traditional Method

1) Cut foundation slightly larger than finished block size plus ½" (1.3 cm) for seam allowances. Cut a patch for one corner; pin in place. Cut another patch to overlap first patch; turn under ¼" (6 mm) on edge that will overlap. Pin or baste in place.

2) Continue to attach patches until foundation is covered. Turn under ¼" (6 mm) on all edges except those on outside of block; pin or baste in place.

3) Stitch along pressed edges, using decorative stitches, working from center to edges; pull needle thread to underside, and knot. Trim the block to the finished size plus ½" (1.3 cm) for seam allowances.

4) Arrange blocks as desired; stitch blocks together into rows. Stitch rows together, finger-pressing seam allowances in opposite directions. Press quilt top. Cut and attach border strips (pages 84 to 89).

5) Cut backing. If batting is desired, cut batting 4" (10 cm) larger than quilt top. Layer and baste quilt top, batting, and backing (pages 96 to 99). Machine-tack or quilt (pages 100 to 109) at frequent intervals. Cut and apply binding (pages 112 and 113).

Alternate method. Follow steps 1 and 2, except overlap patches and do not turn under edges. Stitch over raw edges, using wide decorative stitches; work from center to edges. Trim block to finished size plus ½" (1.3 cm) for seam allowances. Complete quilt as in steps 4 and 5.

How to Make a Crazy Quilt Using the Stitch-and-Flip Method

1) Cut foundation fabric slightly larger than finished block size plus ½" (1.3 cm) for seam allowances. Cut a patch, and place in center or corner of foundation; pin in place. Place a second patch on first patch, right sides together, aligning one edge. Stitch ¼" (6 mm) seam along aligned edges.

2) Flip the second patch right side up; press. Pin in place. Continue to attach patches until foundation is covered; press under ¼" (6 mm) seam allowance on edges that will not be covered.

3) Trim blocks to finished size plus ½" (1.3 cm) for seam allowances. Pin any unstitched folded edges to foundation.

4) Secure unstitched folded edges as for blindstitched appliqué on page 272, step 4. Finish quilt as in steps 4 and 5, opposite. For wall hanging, attach fabric sleeve (page 165). (Contrasting thread was used to show detail.)

More Crazy-quilt Designs

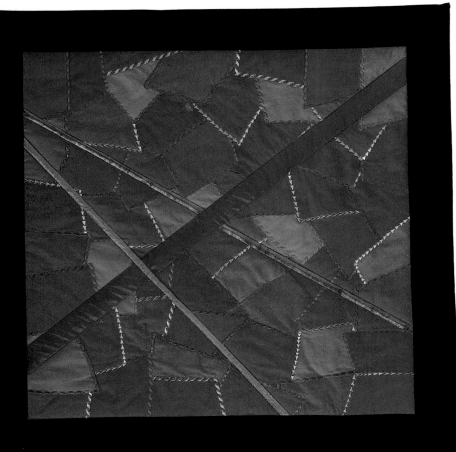

Crazy-quilt variations are limitless. Experiment with any idea, because there are no rules for crazy quilting. For a contemporary look, slash the quilt top and insert a contrasting strip of fabric.

To save time when making a large quilt top, you can alternate patched blocks with plain blocks. Quilt the plain blocks, using a decorative template, to add a new dimension to the quilt.

Contrasting lamé strips have been inserted to give this crazy quilt a contemporary look, and metallic threads were used to carry out the effect. The quilt was made using the traditional method.

How to Add Contrasting Strips to a Crazy-quilt Top

1) Cut insert strip desired finished width plus ½" (1.3 cm). Slash quilt top at desired angle. Subtract ¼" (6 mm) seam allowance from one-half the finished width of insert strip; trim this amount from each slashed edge.

2) Apply interfacing to lamé. Pin and stitch one slashed edge to strip in ¼" (6 mm) seam, with right sides together and insert strip facing up; extend strip beyond ends of block. Press strip right side up.

3) Trim ends of strip even with block. Stitch remaining section of block to opposite side of insert strip, with strip facing up. Repeat steps for additional strips, if desired.

Crazy-quilt blocks and plain blocks have been alternated in this quilt. The plain blocks were quilted using a decorative template. This quilt was made using the stitch-and-flip method.

Pine Trees Placemats & Table Runners

Quilted holiday placemats and a table runner are pieced in a Pine Trees design made from squares and right triangles. The right triangles are quickly and easily cut from fabric strips with the Easy Angle™ cutting tool designed for quilters. If you are not using an Easy Angle cutting tool, cut diagonally across 3⅜" (8.5 cm) fabric squares to make the right triangles.

A table runner can be made to fit any size table. The length of the runner is determined by the number of Pine Trees blocks that are stitched together. The directions that follow are for a runner of four blocks.

The quilt blocks can be constructed from either two or three fabric colors. In the projects shown here, two fabrics are used for the placemats, while the table runner has three fabrics for more variety.

✂ **Cutting Directions** (for one two-color placemat)
From Fabric A, cut four 2½" (6.5 cm) strips across the width of the fabric, to be used for the trees and the binding. From Fabric B, cut three 2½" (6.5 cm) strips across the width of the fabric, to be used for the trees and the background. As shown on page 306, steps 1 and 2, cut 30 triangles from the strips of Fabric A; cut 30 triangles and 18 squares from the strips of Fabric B.

Cut one 13" × 17" (33 × 43 cm) rectangle from the backing fabric and one from batting or fleece.

✂ **Cutting Directions** (for a three-color table runner)
From Fabric A, cut six 2½" (6.5 cm) strips across the width of the fabric, to be used for the trees. From Fabric B, cut four 2½" (6.5 cm) strips across the width of the fabric, to be used for the trees. From Fabric C, cut twelve 2½" (6.5 cm) strips across the width of the fabric, to be used for the background and the binding. As shown on page 306, steps 1 and 2, cut 30 triangles for each tree block from the strips of Fabric A and 18 triangles from the strips of Fabric B; cut 12 triangles and 18 squares for each tree block from the strips of Fabric C.

Cut one 13" × 66" (33 × 168 cm) rectangle from the backing fabric and one from batting or fleece; piece the backing fabric as necessary.

YOU WILL NEED

For four two-color placemats:
1⅓ yd. (1.27 m) **Fabric A,** for trees and binding.
1 yd. (0.95 m) **Fabric B,** for trees and background.
⅞ yd. (0.8 m) backing fabric.
1 yd. (0.95 m) **low-loft quilt batting** or polyester fleece.
Easy Angle cutting tool.

For one three-color table runner:
⅔ yd. (0.63 m) **Fabric A,** for trees.
½ yd. (0.5 m) **Fabric B,** for trees.
1⅛ yd. (1.05 m) **Fabric C,** for background and binding.
⅞ yd. (0.8 m) backing fabric.
2 yd. (1.85 m) **low-loft quilt batting** or polyester fleece.
Easy Angle cutting tool.

Quilted Pine Trees blocks are used to make the table runner and placemats above. Two fabrics are used for the placemats. The third fabric in the table runner gives a dominant Pine Trees effect from both sides.

How to Sew a Pine Trees Placemat

1) Align Easy Angle™ cutting tool with fabric strip at marking for 2½" (6.5 cm) right triangle; cut along diagonal edge of tool.

2) Flip tool over, keeping diagonal edge of tool along diagonal cut of fabric. Align cutting tool with edge of fabric strip at marking for 2½" (6.5 cm) right triangle; cut along straight edge of tool. Continue to cut necessary number of triangles (page 304).

3) Stitch one triangle from Fabric A to one triangle from Fabric B, right sides together, along the long edge, in ¼" (6 mm) seam. Continue piecing triangles until 30 triangle-squares have been completed. Press seams toward tree fabric; trim off points.

4) Stitch background squares and triangle-squares together to make rows, as shown.

5) Stitch rows together, turning seams in opposite directions to reduce bulk. Press seams toward top of tree.

6) Layer backing, batting, and tree block; pin. Quilt tree by stitching over seamlines of tree, stitching in the well of the seam; stitch with hands positioned on either side of presser foot, holding fabric taut.

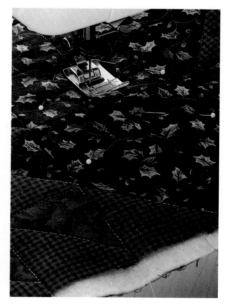

7) Press the binding strip in half lengthwise, wrong sides together. Pin binding strip to right side of the placemat on one long edge, matching raw edges. Stitch ¼" (6 mm) from raw edges.

8) Wrap the binding strip snugly around edge of placemat, covering stitching line on back of placemat; pin. Stitch in the ditch on the right side of the placemat, catching the binding on back side.

9) Stitch the binding strip on the remaining long edge as in steps 7 and 8. Stitch binding strips on the short edges as in step 7; leave ends of binding extending ½" (1.3 cm) beyond the finished edges; secure binding as in step 8, folding ends over finished edges.

How to Sew a Pine Trees Table Runner

1) Follow steps 1 to 4, opposite. In step 3, stitch 18 triangle-squares, joining Fabrics A and B, and 12 triangle-squares, joining Fabrics A and C. Stitch the squares from Fabric C and triangle-squares together to make rows as shown.

2) Complete the block as in step 5, opposite. Make three additional blocks. Stitch the blocks, right sides together, along short edges, in ¼" (6 mm) seams; press. Layer backing, batting, and runner top; pin.

3) Quilt trees as in step 6, opposite. Stitch in the ditch between the tree blocks. Trim batting and backing to match runner top, if necessary. Piece binding strips together on the bias as necessary. Bind edges of runner as in steps 7 to 9.

Christmas Countdown Wall Hangings

Count down the days to Christmas with a Christmas tree wall hanging. Move one miniature ornament from the background to the tree each day beginning December 1 so the tree will be completely decorated by Christmas.

For body, the wall hanging is constructed with a layer of fleece or batting between the front and the back fabric layers. The Christmas tree is appliquéd to the front using a machine satin-stitch. Buttons, stitched to the tree and the background, serve two purposes; they hold the layers together, giving a quilted look, and also hold the ornaments in place.

Hang ornaments in the background area until they are ready to be used on the tree. Display the wall hanging from a rod or dowel, using the tabs across the top.

✂ Cutting Directions

Cut one 26" (66 cm) square each from muslin and fleece or batting.

Cut one 20½" (52.3 cm) square from the fabric for the background.

Cut two 2½" × 20½" (6.5 × 52.3 cm) rectangles from the border fabric, for the upper and lower borders; cut two 2½" × 24½" (6.5 × 62.3 cm) rectangles from the border fabric, for the sides.

Make the pattern for the tree as on page 310, step 1; cut one tree from fabric.

Cut one 2½" × 3" (6.5 × 7.5 cm) rectangle from the fabric for the trunk.

Cut one 24½" (62.3 cm) square from the backing fabric.

Cut four 2½" × 4½" (6.5 × 11.5 cm) rectangles from the border fabric, for the tabs.

YOU WILL NEED

⅔ yd. (0.63 m) fabric, for background.

⅓ yd. (0.32 m) fabric, for border.

½ yd. (0.5 m) fabric, for tree.

¾ yd. (0.7 m) muslin.

¾ yd. (0.7 m) fabric, for backing.

¾ yd. (0.7 m) fleece or batting.

Tear-away stabilizer.

Scrap of fabric for tree trunk.

Forty-eight buttons.

Twenty-four miniature tree ornaments, about 1" (2.5 cm) long.

One star ornament or button, for top of tree.

1" (2.5 cm) grid, such as cutting mat or graph paper.

Rod or dowel, up to ½" (1.3 cm) in diameter.

Diagram for the Tree

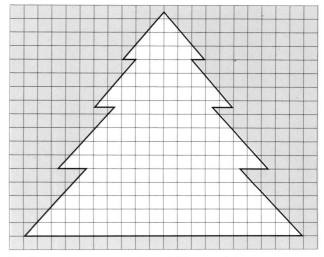

Scale: one square on the grid is equal to one square inch (2.5 sq. cm).

How to Sew a Christmas Countdown Wall Hanging

1) Place tracing paper over a 1" (2.5 cm) grid, such as a cutting mat. Make a full-size pattern for the tree, using diagram (page 309); enlarge tree, using grid lines as a guide. Cut the tree from fabric.

2) Center the 3" (7.5 cm) width of the trunk on background fabric at the lower edge; secure with glue stick. Appliqué sides of trunk to background.

3) Center tree on fabric, over trunk, 2¼" (6 cm) above lower edge; secure with pins or glue stick. Appliqué tree to background.

4) Place muslin square on the work surface; cover with fleece. Center the background fabric over fleece. Pin-baste layers together.

5) Pin around the tree through all layers. Stitch around outer edge of tree along satin stitching, to define outline of tree.

6) Pin the upper and lower border strips to background fabric, right sides together; stitch ¼" (6 mm) from edges through all layers. Turn borders right side up; pin to fleece and muslin layers.

7) Repeat step 6 for the side border strips. Baste close to outer edges of border through all layers. Trim off excess batting and muslin.

8) Secure star ornament or button to top of tree. Stitch 24 buttons to background and 24 buttons to tree, spacing them evenly.

9) Fold one tab in half, right sides together; stitch ¼" (6 mm) seam along edge opposite fold. Turn tab right side out; press, centering the seam on back of tab. Repeat for remaining tabs.

10) Fold tabs in half, with seams to inside, matching raw edges; press. Pin tabs to upper edge on right side of wall hanging front, placing one tab ¼" (6 mm) from each side and spacing remaining tabs evenly across the top; baste.

11) Pin wall hanging front to backing fabric, right sides together. Stitch ¼" (6 mm) from raw edges, leaving 12" (30.5 cm) opening for turning; trim the corners. Turn the wall hanging right side out; press. Slipstitch opening closed.

Quilted Placemats & Table Runners

This placemat and table runner set is sewn using a machine-quilting method called "quilt-as-you-go." In this method, the batting is layered over the backing fabric, and the quilt pieces are sewn through the layers, piecing and quilting the project at the same time.

A single Square-in-a-Square Quilt Block is used for each placemat, with a border strip on each short end. The table runner consists of several quilt blocks, sewn in a row, with border strips at the ends of the runner and between the blocks.

The 11½" (29.3 cm) quilt block, combined with two 3" (7.5 cm) border strips, makes a finished placemat that measures about 11½" × 17½" (29.3 × 44.3 cm). The table runner, made from four quilt blocks and five strips, measures about 11½" × 61" (29.3 × 155 cm). To vary the length of the table runner, use a different number of quilt blocks or change the width of the strips at the ends and between the blocks.

Select five coordinating fabrics for piecing the quilt blocks. From the center out to the edges of the block, the fabrics are referred to as Fabric A through Fabric E. The yardage requirements at right are for either a set of four placemats or for one table runner.

Use a stitch length of 12 to 15 stitches per inch (2.5 cm). When piecing the fabrics together, it is not necessary to backstitch, because each seam will be intersected by another seam in the following step. Use an Even Feed® foot or walking foot, if available, to help prevent the layers from shifting as you sew.

✂ Cutting Directions (for one placemat)

From Fabric A, cut one 3⅜" (8.5 cm) square for the center square of the placemat, and cut two 3½" × 12" (9 × 30.5 cm) border strips.

From Fabric B, cut two 2⅞" (7.2 cm) squares; cut the squares in half diagonally, to make four triangles.

From Fabric C, cut two 3¾" (9.5 cm) squares; cut the squares in half diagonally, to make four triangles.

From Fabric C, also cut two 2" (5 cm) strips across the full width of the fabric, to be used for the binding.

From Fabric D, cut two 4⅞" (12.2 cm) squares; cut the squares in half diagonally, to make four triangles.

From Fabric E, cut two 6½" (16.3 cm) squares; cut the squares in half diagonally, to make four triangles.

Cut one 14" × 20" (35.5 × 51 cm) rectangle each from backing fabric and batting.

✂ Cutting Directions (for one table runner)

For each quilt block in the table runner, cut fabric squares and triangles from Fabrics A through E, following the cutting directions for one placemat. From Fabric A, also cut five 3½" × 12" (9 × 30.5 cm) border strips. From Fabric C, also cut four 2" (5 cm) strips across the full width of the fabric, to be used for the binding.

Cut one 14" × 20" (35.5 × 51 cm) rectangle each from backing fabric and batting. Cut three 14" × 17" (35.5 × 43 cm) rectangles each from backing fabric and batting. Cut the wide bias tape into three 12" (30.5 cm) lengths.

YOU WILL NEED

For four placemats or one table runner:

½ yd. (0.5 m) **Fabric A,** to be used for center of quilt block and for border strips.

¼ yd. (0.25 m) **Fabric B.**

½ yd. (0.5 m) **Fabric C,** to be used for pieces of quilt block and for binding edges.

¼ yd. (0.25 m) **Fabric D.**

½ yd. (0.5 m) **Fabric E.**

1 yd. (0.95 m) **backing fabric.**

Lightweight polyester quilt batt, in crib-quilt size, rinsed and machine dried.

1 yd. (0.95 m) **wide bias tape** to match backing fabric, for table runner only.

How to Sew a Quilted Placemat

1) Mark lines through center of the batting, in both directions, using lead pencil. Layer batting over backing, matching edges; pin in place.

2) Fold the center square of Fabric A in half, in both directions; finger-press center marks along each side. Place square flat at center of placemat, matching center of each side to marked lines on batting. Pin in place, with heads of pins toward center of square.

3) Place one triangle from Fabric B on the center square, right sides together, with diagonally cut side of triangle even with one side of square. At ends, allow points of triangle to extend equal distances beyond corners of square. Sew 1/4" (6 mm) seam through all layers.

4) Turn the triangle right side up, finger-pressing along the seamline. Align point of triangle with marked line on batting; pin in place.

5) Repeat steps 3 and 4 for opposite side of square, then for remaining sides, using triangles from Fabric B.

6) Place ruler diagonally across center square; mark line on batting, using lead pencil. Repeat in opposite diagonal direction.

7) Apply set of triangles from Fabric C as in steps 3 to 5, aligning center of each triangle to marked line. Stitching lines should intersect the corners of center square exactly.

8) Continue in same manner for the set of triangles from Fabric D, then for triangles from Fabric E. Stitch one border strip to each side of placemat, aligning center of strip with corner of triangle in quilt block.

9) Smooth the border strips toward the outer edges of placemat. With a straightedge along edge of quilt block, trim excess fabric, batting, and backing, using rotary cutter. Or mark a line, and trim the layers with shears.

10) Press binding strips in half lengthwise, wrong sides together.

(Continued on next page)

How to Sew a Quilted Placemat (continued)

11) Pin one folded binding strip to one long edge of the placemat top, matching raw edges, with end of strip extending 1" (2.5 cm) beyond end of the placemat. Stitch a scant ¼" (6 mm) from raw edges.

12) Wrap the binding strip snugly around edge of placemat, covering stitching line on back of placemat. From placemat top, pin in the ditch of the seam.

13) Stitch in the ditch on placemat top by stitching over the seamline in the well of the seam; catch the binding on the back of the placemat in the stitching.

14) Repeat steps 11 to 13 for opposite long edge of placemat. Trim ends of upper and lower binding strips even with edges of placemat.

15) Repeat step 11 for shorter ends of placemat. Trim ends of binding strips to extend ½" (1.3 cm) beyond finished edges of placemat.

16) Fold ½" (1.3 cm) end of the binding over finished edge; press in place. Wrap binding to back of placemat and stitch as in steps 12 and 13. Slipstitch ends.

How to Sew a Quilted Table Runner

1) Mark 14" × 20" (35.5 × 51 cm) rectangle of quilt batting as on page 314, step 1; mark the three 14" × 17" (35.5 × 43 cm) rectangles of batting horizontally through center, and vertically 2" (5 cm) to one side of center. Layer batting pieces over backing pieces, matching the edges.

2) Stitch the quilt blocks as on pages 314 and 315, steps 2 to 9, stitching border strips to both short ends of the large rectangle and to one short end of the smaller rectangles.

3) Pin the large rectangle to one smaller rectangle along the end without the border strip, right sides together. Stitch ¼" (6 mm) seam through all layers.

4) Join the remaining quilt blocks for the table runner as in step 3, left. Trim batting from seam allowances on back of the table runner.

5) Pin one length of bias tape to back of the runner, centered over a seam; hand-stitch in place, catching backing fabric only. Repeat for all remaining seams. Trim ends of bias tape even with edges of runner.

6) Apply binding to table runner as on pages 315 and 316, steps 10 to 16.

Index

Cowles Creative Publishing, Inc. offers a variety of how-to books. For information write:

Cowles Creative Publishing
Subscriber Books
5900 Green Oak Drive
Minnetonka, MN 55343